KNITTING DETAILS
START TO FINISH

A HANDBOOK OF SIMPLE TRICKS, CREATIVE SOLUTIONS, AND FINISHING TECHNIQUES

by Ulla Engquist

TRAFALGAR SQUARE
North Pomfret, Vermont

*A big thank you to my family who put up
with me when I was always knitting!
Thank you, Karin and Gunnel.*

First published in the United States of America
in 2016 by
Trafalgar Square Books
North Pomfret, Vermont 05053

Originally published in Swedish as *Sticka—detaljer som gör skillnad.*

Copyright © 2015 Hemslöjdens forlag
English translation © 2016 Trafalgar Square Books

ISBN: 978-1-57076-783-8   **33614057811993**

Library of Congress Control Number: 2016955565

Photography Thomas Harrysson
Illustrations Eva Riise
Knitted samples Ulla Engquist
Interior designer Cecilia Ljungström
Original publisher Ulrika Rapp
Editor Cecilia Ljungström
Technical Editors Karin Kahnlund and Gunnel Andersson
Translator Carol Huebscher Rhoades

Printed in China
10 9 8 7 6 5 4 3 2 1

CONTENTS

PREFACE

Sitting down with your knitting and working stitch after stitch brings balance into your existence. Your thoughts wander, you remember the past and imagine the future, and the good and bad, the easy and the difficult, are worked into your garment.

Knitting has always been a central part of my life. As far back as I can remember, I've always had some knitting in progress—not necessarily a garment, but often something I've wanted to try out or solve a technical problem on. Later on, this knitting was part of preparing workshop materials.

My paternal grandmother taught me how to knit when I was four years old and I began with a stocking leg! Despite that, this book doesn't have anything about socks, even though there's a lot of exciting things to say on that subject. Instead, this book is concerned with the beautiful art of assembling and finishing—an invisible shoulder seam, a discreet increase, or a pretty neckband are the details that take a garment to the next level and make it look really good!

Maybe you are one of those crafters who likes to knit but has never quite understood how to assemble a piece. In this book, I share the experience I've accumulated in that area over the years. It's not about employing complicated solutions, but rather tried-and-true methods that will be easy for you to pick up and learn.

Be curious and dare to experiment! Try out various cast-on methods and edges, test-knit the details, and figure out which bind-off you like the best. Certainly it takes patience to produce a neat and supple Kitchener stitch seam, but fine and well-thought-out finishing elevates the whole garment.

Good luck!
Ulla Engquist

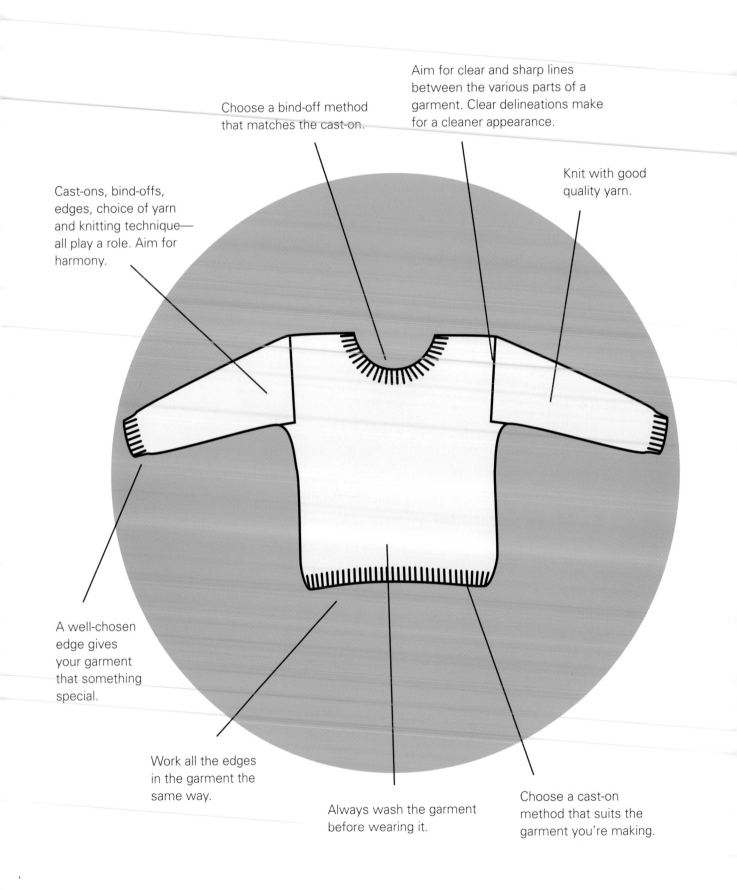

Choose a bind-off method that matches the cast-on.

Aim for clear and sharp lines between the various parts of a garment. Clear delineations make for a cleaner appearance.

Knit with good quality yarn.

Cast-ons, bind-offs, edges, choice of yarn and knitting technique—all play a role. Aim for harmony.

A well-chosen edge gives your garment that something special.

Work all the edges in the garment the same way.

Always wash the garment before wearing it.

Choose a cast-on method that suits the garment you're making.

Introduction

When I'm about to design a sweater, I want it to be pretty and exhibit an aesthetic wholeness. I usually imagine a circle and place the sweater inside the circle. The yarn quality, color choice, knitting technique, cast-on method, edges, bind-offs, increases, decreases, buttons, and other finishing details—all should coordinate and fit inside the circle; nothing should fall out.

A sweater with the sleeve cuffs knitted in one technique, the lower edge of the body in another technique, and the neckband in yet a third style makes a very uneven impression, especially if the knitting on the rest of the garment is patterned. The potential for collective, thought-through completeness is lost, and you'll have an unfortunate result. The various parts of the sweater don't belong inside the same circle.

In order to successfully create a harmonious whole, it's important to plan your knitting from the very beginning and decide how to handle the small details that will make the knitted garment something special.

The little details depend on the larger parts as well as the garment's finishing. Finishing is, unfortunately, a word that sounds a little negative to many knitters. Perhaps you belong to that group that knits happily but makes a face when it's time for the final details. No need for that! Finishing is fun when you know all the little tricks, and they aren't at all difficult.

FINISHING SHOULD BE DONE BUT NOT SEEN

Sometimes you look at a sweater and see there's something special about it, but you can't quite put your finger on what it is that makes it so nice. All the little finishing details should be made as consistently and discreetly as possible. Keep in mind that the inside should also look neat!

There are several important techniques that you should know: knitting the edge stitches, sewing the side seams, grafting, making increases and decreases, binding off neatly, and calculating the ratio between the stitches and rows. With all this in hand, you'll go a long way.

For me, it's always important that there are clear and straight lines in the knitting. For knitting, this means—among other things—that when you pick up and knit stitches or graft inside the edge stitches, you do so without catching in the next stitch. The transition between the knitting and other edges that will be picked up and knitted afterwards will have a prettier and cleaner look when the transition forms a sharp line—the garment will have character and be distinct.

It's not always the most difficult or complex pattern that gives the best end result or the prettiest effect in a garment. A lovely yarn, good technique, and gauge suitable for the composition; a well-thought-out choice of edges, cast-on, and bind-off methods; and carefully-selected buttons, or another form of closure all make a garment lovely without any of the individual parts being complicated. You can also decide how to add other personal embellishments to the final result.

INSTRUCTIONS IN THE BOOK

Throughout this book, the instructions are written so you can choose a yarn you like and knit samples of increases, various cast-on methods, and neckbands, for example. Use a light and even yarn so it will be easier to work and the results will be obvious.

The samples shown in the book have, in many cases, been finished with yarn of a different color to illustrate the work better. For example, on certain neckbands I decided to pick up and knit stitches with yarn of a contrasting color, or to carry a strand of contrast-color sewing thread together with the yarn for the picking-up row. I have even sewn a short stretch of duplicate stitch on the inside of the neckband with a contrast color. This is to show where and how the stitches are placed and how they integrate with the rest of the piece. You can also see how I let stitches sit on a holder, as they do when an edge with live stitches will be sewn down.

Of course, the sewing thread won't be there when you knit an actual garment and you'll sew with the same color as for the rest of the knitting. It's only shown that way here so you can see how it's done.

The sweaters and all the technique swatches in this book are intended to inspire your knitting and creativity. For each sample or sweater, I've listed what type of cast-on, edge, increases, decreases, bind-off, and so forth were used. I'm sure you have a basic pattern somewhere in your collection—get it out and choose some yarn, a good cast-on, a suitable edge, and finishing. For every stage of the finishing, you'll find easy tips in the text with accompanying photos and drawings.

The swatches and sweaters in this book were knitted with Rauma Finullgarn (CYCA #1, 100% wool, 191 yd/175 m / 50 g). For stockinette stitch, I used needles U.S. size 2.5 / 3 mm and, for most of the edges, U.S. size 1.5 / 2.5 mm. The gauge is 26 stitches and 39 rows in 4 x 4 in / 10 x 10 cm.

PLANNING YOUR KNITTING

When you're about to knit a garment, you should always start by planning. Take your time, sit down in peace and quiet, and read through all the instructions. It will be worth the extra time you spent when you actually start knitting.

Have paper, pen, and a little mini-calculator at hand. Note what needs to be adjusted to make it better without changing the pattern. This might have to do with edges, pattern matching at the sides as well as at the neckband and armholes, buttons, buttonhole bands, placement and function of buttonholes, armhole depth in relation to the number of stitches on the sleeves, circular vs knitting back and forth, edge stitches—yes, there's a lot to consider!

If you don't want to change the pattern or you aren't confident enough to want to risk it right away (understandable!), you should still carefully read through all the instructions before you start. You'll almost never follow a pattern in precise chronological order. One step might need to be described clearly before the next one can be worked. In practical terms, this can mean that you have to begin a new detail before you are totally finished with a previous one, and in the end you work both simultaneously. Knowing where and when this happens in the pattern and being prepared will make it much easier to get a good result.

Useful Tips

＊ When you are going to bind off, graft stitches, or knit a row, it's good to know how much yarn you need for that step. Estimate about four times as much yarn as the width of the knitting. For the side seams, calculate three times the length, but add a little extra for some leeway as you work.

＊ When grafting or sewing side seams, you should pull out the length of yarn needed for the seams right at the beginning so the yarn end is in place and you won't have to weave in extra yarn later on.

＊ A small see-through magnifying ruler is the best tool to use for counting stitches and rows and an excellent aid for controlling gauge.

＊ For finishing, you should use various sizes of needles depending on what you're doing. A blunt tapestry needle, preferably with a curved tip, is used for sewing up side seams and duplicate or Kitchener stitch. This type of needle minimizes the risk that you'll catch a strand where you shouldn't. A sharp-pointed needle is used for weaving in ends because the needle has to go through the yarn plies.

The size of the needle should be suited to the knitting; that is to say, if you used a heavy yarn, you need a bigger needle, and if you used thin yarn, use a finer needle.

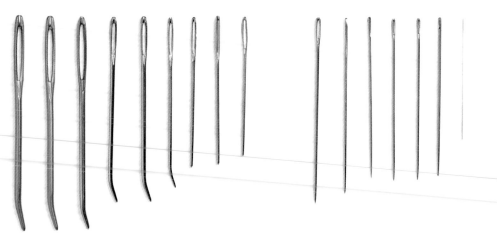

There are different types of needles for various purposes.

＊ If you have to rip out some knitting, it's important to take out the entire row and knit it again from the beginning for a smoother result. If you only rip out a little of the row, you can end up with long, uneven stitches at the center of the piece. If a large section has to be ripped out and redone, it's smart to pick up the stitches with the knitting needle when one row remains before the restart row and then rip back stitch by stitch—this keeps all the stitches in the right order. This method is particularly good if you have a difficult pattern, uneven yarn, or tricky edge stitches.

＊ If you need to look for a mistake in the knitting, find an increase or a decrease, or see how much of a caught strand is visible, hold the knitting up to a lamp or in sunlight. This will help you see the details more clearly.

＊ Sometimes it's easier to check the wrong side to follow or count the rows in stockinette, a texture pattern, or something similar.

＊ Sometimes it's more difficult to keep the purl or wrong side rows in stockinette even and at the same tension as for the knit rows. One way to control this problem is to use a smaller (1 U.S. size / ½ mm) needle for these rows. Another alternative is to change your grip (the way you hold the needles) or to adjust the yarn tension. You can let the yarn loop over your forefinger and hang in your palm, letting the other fingers hold onto it. If this doesn't work, try weaving the yarn over your forefinger, under the middle finger, over the ring finger, and under the little finger, which you can also wrap the yarn around. If the problem still persists, try working around on a circular needle—using only knit stitches. You can knit the body up the neck this way and then cut openings for the armholes and neck. Try each method to see what works best for you.

＊ Make sure that you never start clutching the stitches in your right hand, because the knitting can easily become uneven. Let the stitches sit freely on the needle.

* If you have pain in your shoulders and arms when you knit, try working back and forth on a circular needle instead of straights. The weight of the piece will fall on your knees or in your lap instead of at the ends of the needles, where it quickly becomes heavy to work with.

* When you take a break from your knitting, some yarns might slacken their tension a little, which means that the next time you begin to knit, the first stitches might be a little large and uneven. Get into the habit of always knitting to the end of a row and "locking in" the yarn with a few firm wraps around the needle. When working in the round, leave off at one "side," and secure the yarn with a few firm wraps around the needle. Don't forget to remove the extra wraps when you start knitting again.

* For some of us, the stitches tend to be a little looser at the end of a row. To compensate for that, try knitting the first four or five stitches at the beginning of the row a little more firmly. Then, when you come to those stitches on the next row, you'll have carried a little extra yarn across the whole row and the firm stitches will loosen a little. If you don't knit them more firmly at the beginning, the stitches could become obviously longer.

* To further decrease the risk of unevenness in knitting, it's a good idea to try and knit the garment without taking long breaks from it or knitting several other projects in between. You'll get the best results if you remember what you had planned from the beginning, so the yarn, needles, and grip you're using to maintain the yarn tension will be the same throughout the project.

* If it's hard to, for example, follow the row in a knitted piece when you need to sew down a folded edge, or to see the stitches when you are grafting, you can work a contrast-color sewing thread in with the yarn as you knit. Remove the sewing thread afterwards.

* If you are knitting with black yarn and have trouble seeing the details in the piece, lay a white towel on your knee. It will add contrast and extra light. An alternative is to sit so light falls diagonally from the back and the left.

✳ Use a camera as an extra eye. Sometimes the camera lens will help distinguish what your eye misses—unevenness in the knitting, or color changes in the yarn.

✳ What needles best suit the yarn? To check this, take a needle and make a hole with it through a piece of paper (or use a ruler with holes for needle sizes) and then try to thread the yarn through the hole. If the yarn matches the diameter of the hole, you are ready to begin a *gauge swatch*.

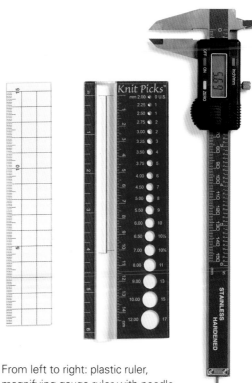

From left to right: plastic ruler, magnifying gauge ruler with needle sizing, and a vernier caliper.

✳ When the instructions mention a right and left front, you have to imagine the garment on your body. The right front is the piece that sits on the right front side of your body.

✳ When there's mention of right- and left-leaning increases and decreases, this right and left is relative to the piece as it's held in front of you in your hands while you knit. The same applies to edges, sides, and so on.

✳ Keep in mind that knitted garments can become worn and lose their shape if you regularly carry a shoulder bag. This happens even if the strap is smooth or the bag is light.

✳ Always wash your garments before you start wearing them.

In the Knitter's Basket

Just so you'll always have all your knitting tools at hand, it's a good idea to assemble them in a basket. Here's what you need:

* Assortment of needle sizes and lengths—if there's room.

* Assortment of crochet hook sizes.

* Scissors.

* Notebook and pen.

* Sewing needles/sewing pins.

* Safety pins.

* Pointed tip tapestry needles.

* Blunt tip tapestry needles, preferably with a curved tip.

* Magnifying ruler.

* Measuring tape.

* Ruler or vernier caliper (there are digital versions).

* A hank of mercerized cotton yarn, for example size 8/4.

* Black and white cotton sewing thread.

* Mini-calculator.

* White towel.

* Assortment of stitch markers.

* Cork, rubber bands, or plastic beads to cap one end of short needles.

Seven Basics of Finishing

In order to be able to finish a piece of knitting, there are seven important steps that you should consider before you even cast on. With these starting points, you can achieve a good result and, afterwards, learn even more. The basics are:

1 Edge stitches.

2 Side seams.

3 Grafting.

4 Increases.

5 Decreases.

6 The ratio of stitches and rows.

7 Binding-off.

The Sequence for Finishing a Simple Sweater

1 Seam the sides.

2 Seam the sleeves.

3 Seam the shoulders with Kitchener stitch or three-needle bind-off.

4 Mark the center of the sleeve cap at the top and count the stitches.

5 Attach the sleeves by grafting.

6 Make sure that the armhole seams are centered.

7 Pick up and knit stitches around the neck.

8 Knit the neckband and bind off.

9 Weave in all ends as neatly and invisibly as possible.

10 Wash the garment and leave it until dry.

Yarn

Decide the purpose of the garment—sturdy or fine—before you choose the yarn. Always use good quality yarn—your time will be the same no matter what quality yarn you use but the appearance, before and after wearing, will vary depending on the yarn. Perhaps you have a fine old sweater in your dresser that has only become finer through many years of wear? That tells you that the materials were first class. No matter what materials you use, you must always make a gauge swatch and block the swatch before you start knitting.

Sweaters knitted with wool yarn are both warm and strong. Wool has unique qualities that allow it to be warm even when damp, a quality which has contributed to saving the lives of many sailors.

A garment made with alpaca yarn is both stronger and warmer than one made of wool and it will also be nice and cool when it's warm outside. However, a multi-color pattern knitted with alpaca yarn will not work well; choose wool for that kind of knitting instead. Alpaca has a tendency to "go out on its own," whereas wool tends to hold the stitches in better because wool fibers hook into each other. Knit more firmly whenever you are working with alpaca yarn.

For textured patterns it's best, as a general rule, to use a multi-ply wool yarn, preferably one that is round and maintains its quality.

Use mercerized cotton whenever you are knitting with cotton yarn. The yarn will have been processed with cold hydroxide, stretched, and dried so the yarn has a lovely luster and shine. Keep in mind that cotton yarn is rather heavy, so choose patterns and techniques that work well with the yarn's characteristics, and knit more firmly than usual. Cotton garments don't expel moisture well, so they can feel damp against the body.

Linen can be a little hard to handle; you may end up fighting with the yarn at times. It's not a material I would recommend for beginners. However, linen absorbs moisture well and expels it quickly, so it's a lovely material for summer wear.

Silk is a material with a fantastic luster and feel, and another fabric that will be cool and pleasant in summer. Unfortunately, a sweater knitted with silk will have a tendency to stretch in the first wash, so it's very

important to knit swatches and wash them before deciding on the stitch count, number of rows, technique, and sizing.

Cotton, linen, and silk are all what you might call "inelastic" materials. You have to take that into consideration when you choose an edging strategy. Instead of regular ribbing, you might need to work a twisted rib of some sort. Even when weaving in ends, you need to do so in a special way so the yarn won't slide out (see page 22).

If you're a beginner and haven't knitted very much, I recommend you start with a somewhat firm, "roundly plied" yarn in a light color. That style of yarn will make it easier to see what you're doing—and while any unevenness will be more obvious with a light color of yarn, most of that will disappear in the first wash, and you should always wash a garment before you start wearing it.

Some single-ply yarns have a tendency to bias when knitted with certain techniques, such as stockinette. You should, instead, try a technique in which the purl and knit stitches counteract each other—seed stitch is one option. You should always knit back and forth with single-ply yarns.

When you're going to knit a sweater, you should always buy a little extra yarn. Partly because you'll need to knit gauge swatches before you begin the sweater, and partly because it's good to have a little leftover yarn for future use. Perhaps you'll need to lengthen or repair the sweater, or knit new edges. You never know!

Always save the pattern instructions and a yarn ball band together with the yarn. Also save all the gauge swatches and your notes about stitch and row counts, how you cast on and bound off, which needles you used for what parts of the garment, etc. Even if it seems a little ambitious, it's a good idea to record anything special you did, any changes or adjustments you made, and what worked well and what didn't. By doing this, you'll learn more and develop your skills.

INELASTIC YARNS AND KNITTING

If you're working with any yarn that is inelastic or a little uneven in structure, or you're knitting with a fine yarn and working a slippery type of knitting, you have to consider this when you choose the edges and work very carefully when finishing. Linen is a good example of a yarn that needs a little more attention from you when you are knitting. Here are a few tips.

Try knitting the edge with a reversible, twisted ribbing. Choose either k1, p1 or k2, p2 ribbing. Inelastic yarns hold this type of ribbing rather well and it has a nice effect. Use the same size needles as for regular ribbing.

With fine linen yarn, it's also a good idea to work folded edges in stockinette or to knit a narrow edge with garter stitch as a frame.

If you don't want to have an edge, it's fine to just delineate the opening by picking up and knitting stitches around the neck and armholes and then binding off on the first row. You could also knit a stockinette row before binding off, which produces a somewhat different appearance. This type of edge on a lighter garment makes it look well-worked and it holds the knitting together well.

When seaming a shoulder with this type of yarn, I recommend that you leave live stitches on both the back and front and join them with Kitchener stitch. If you bind off the back, it can leave a clumpy stripe centered over the shoulder on, for example, an otherwise sheer summer linen.

Think about …

… how all yarns can offer big surprises when the garment is finished if you don't block your little gauge swatch before you start knitting!

WINDING YARN

Wool yarn should always be wound loosely to maintain the yarn's elasticity and loft. If you wind it too firmly, the yarn will stretch—and then return to its proper length in the knitted garment. Wind all the yarn for a project at the same time so you'll be handling it all the same way.

Wind all the skeins the same way. Begin from the same end and remove the yarn from the ball in the same direction. Always begin knitting with the same end from each ball—either from the inside or the outside. One ball with the yarn pulled from the opposite direction can affect the twist in the yarn as well as the finished result, with various rows in the garment looking different. The same rule also applies to yarn bought in balls: Always begin knitting from the same yarn end.

Sometimes, you might notice that the yarn twists as you knit—if so, try knitting from the opposite end (but not if you've already begun working on other parts of the same garment). To avoid having to worry about this, you can do a simple test before you start knitting. Take out one end, wrap the yarn firmly around your index and middle fingers a few times, drop the yarn and, with both hands, quickly grab each end of the yarn; bring your hands together to make a loop with the yarn. Do the same test with the other end of the yarn. The end that twists the *least* is the end to start knitting with.

According to the experts, you should begin knitting with the section of the yarn that, as raw material, was first fed into the spinning machine.

DIFFERENT YARN DYELOTS IN THE SAME GARMENT

If you're almost at the end of your yarn and you have to continue knitting with yarn of another dyelot, you can minimize the effects of the color shift by knitting one row with the new yarn, three rows with the old, two rows with the new, two rows with the old, three rows with the new, one row with the old before completely changing to the new dyelot. It's even better if you can make this change in an area where it won't be very visible. You might also be able to add a knit row that will draw the eye away from the color shift, or change dyelots within a multi-color pattern.

Try not to change dyelots on a sleeve or front—if you do, then change the yarns the same way on both fronts or sleeves so the color shift will blend in with the pattern as a whole and look natural. If you have enough of the new dyelot to use for all the bands and edges, then the problem is solved!

SPLICING AND WEAVING IN YARNS

If you need to splice the yarn, you should do so at the side of the garment. You should never have knots in your knitting! It's very hard to make them completely invisible, and they might pop out and make a hole. Splicing yarn by splitting the plies, thinning them out, moistening the ends, and rubbing them together should also not be done on a garment. The yarn usually loses its twist and this can be clearly seen in the knitting. The only time you should splice yarn this way is when sewing a side seam—the yarn won't be visible then.

When it's time to weave in ends, it's always best and easiest to do so at the edge stitches. Use a sharp-tipped needle; bring the needle down centered on the line of the outermost edge stitch, into the center of the yarn plies. Insert the needle about 1¼ in / 3 cm through the knitting, bring the yarn through and make a stitch about ³⁄₈ in / 1 cm back into the same part of the stitch. Trim the yarn about ³⁄₈ in / 1 cm from the knitting. When you wear the garment later on, the yarn has room to move and the trimmed end will gradually blend in.

Think about ...

✳ The exact length of yarn needed for weaving in varies depending on the yarn fiber. Wool yarn, which is grabby, doesn't need a long strand for weaving in, while silk, linen, or mercerized cotton that can easily slide out might need to be woven in differently. In that case, you can reinforce the weaving in with a few extra stitches. See photos on page 22.

✳ If you are knitting in the round with doubled yarn, do not change out both strands at the same time. Make sure there are a couple of inches / a few centimeters in between each.

PHOTO 1 Stockinette stitch, example of how to weave in on one "side" of circular kntting.
PHOTO 2 Ribbing, example of how to weave in on one "side" of circular knitting.
PHOTO 3 Garter stitch, example of how to weave in horizontally between two ridges.

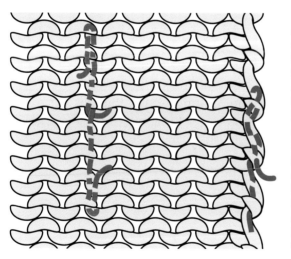

Stockinette Stitch. The yarn is woven in through edge stitches and at the "side" on a circularly knitted piece into a *vertical* line of stitches. The ends are fastened off each in their own direction.

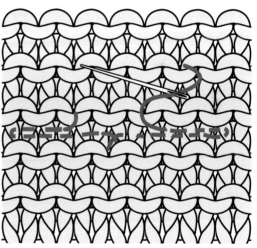

Garter Stitch. The yarn is woven in *horizontally* below a ridge on the wrong side. The ends are fastened off each in their own direction.

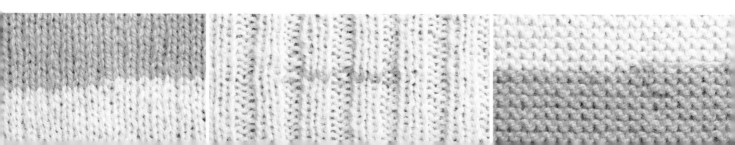

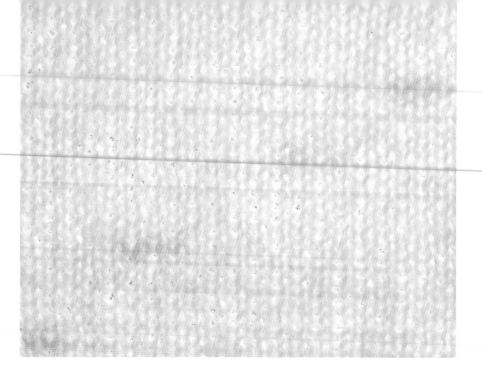

ABOVE Here you can see where the yarns were spliced by the moistening and rubbing method. This method is not recommended. The splices are visible as dark, horizontal splotches.

BELOW Silk. Stockinette Stitch, example of how to weave in ends vertically along the edge stitches at the side and centered on a "side" in circular knitting. You can make it easier to see by holding a strand of contrast color sewing thread with the yarn if necessary. The seam should be neat and not at all visible on the right side.

I usually wait until it's time for finishing to weave in all the ends on a garment. At that point, it's usually easier to see the neatest and least visible places. Weaving in ends for a side piece before the side seam is joined can make it difficult to see the edge stitches.

When joining yarns in a circularly knitted stockinette knit piece, there are no edge stitches to weave yarn into. You should instead weave in the yarn right at the side along one vertical line of stitches, precisely where the stitches catch onto each other—but not in the center of a stitch or between two stitches. Sew as described above, one yarn end upwards and one down, overlapping the yarns (do not knot them) on the wrong side to avoid holes. The lower yarn is woven upwards and the upper one downwards. Make sure they're not visible on the right side.

If you have worked back and forth in garter stitch, you can weave in the yarn at the side or horizontally under a ridge on the wrong side. Run the needle right below each ridge, in the part that forms a ridge on the right side. Look on the right side to see how it looks before you pull the needle through or cut the yarn. Hold the knitting up to the light to see your results better.

RIPPED YARN

When you rip out knitting, you may find the yarn has "set" and become uneven, and therefore unsuitable to continue knitting with. If you knit with yarn that has been ripped out, the results will not be even and smooth. If you want to use some yarn that has already been knitted with, you have to refresh the yarn. Begin by winding the yarn into a skein and lightly securing the skein with figure eight strands of cotton knotted in at four places around the skein to avoid tangles. Dampen the yarn, stretch it out a little, and let it dry. Now you can knit with the yarn again. Try to remember what end you started with before so you can begin there again (see Winding Yarn on page 19).

Needles

It's important to use good quality knitting needles. Don't work with needles with damaged tips or circulars that don't have a smooth connection between cord and needle.

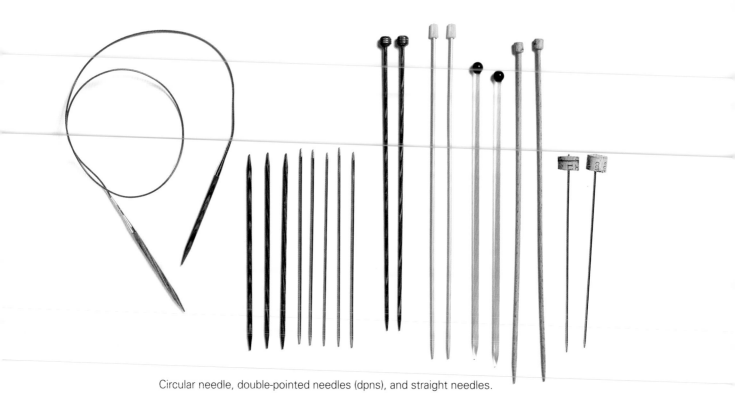

Circular needle, double-pointed needles (dpns), and straight needles.

If you're knitting with different sizes of needle in the same garment, make sure all the needles are from the same company and made with the same material. There can be small differences in needles from different manufacturers even if the needles are supposed to be the same size. It's also different knitting with wood or plywood needles than with smooth metal or plastic needles. If you use different types of needles for one garment, you might grip them differently—you'll tend to adjust your grip for each kind of needle, and then your knitting will be uneven.

Certain types of needle can sometimes be a little rough. If you rub them with a little stearin, the stitches will slide along more easily and your knitting will go more quickly.

Wood needles and synthetic fiber yarn do not go together. The stitches will move slowly along the needle and it will be hard to work.

Sometimes it can be a little tricky to get hold of the stitches when binding off or picking up stitches on, for example, a neckband. If you use a more pointed needle, the job will be easier.

When you are putting your knitting aside, you should never insert the needles into the ball of yarn or into the knitted fabric. You'll cause ugly marks in your knitting. No matter how smooth and fine your needles are, the yarn can split or rip.

If you are knitting a somewhat smaller garment, it's often more practical to use double-pointed needles instead of straights. To prevent the stitches from falling off the end of a double-pointed needle, you can stick a bit of cork on one end as a stopper. Cut the cork into reasonably sized pieces, bring some water to boil, and let the cork pieces soak in the water for a while. Remove the cork from the water and stop the needle ends while the cork is still warm. As the cork dries, it will shrink and form a firm stop. Alternately, you can wrap a rubber band around or pop a plastic bead onto the needle end.

Sometimes the cords on circular needles can be quite hard and look like a spiral, which makes it hard to hold the needles and makes knitting difficult. The problem can be easily solved by either pouring hot water on the cord or blowing on it with a hair dryer until it softens. Use your left hand to grab one needle tip and straighten out the cord with your right hand at the same time. After it cools, the cord should be straight and neat.

Gauge Swatch

Before you begin knitting, it's very important to read through the instructions and make a gauge swatch. This applies to all the knitting techniques included in the project. Always cast on a few more stitches and work a few more rows than required for a square of 4 x 4 in / 10 x 10 cm. These extra stitches and rows will make things easier for you when it comes to measuring the gauge swatch.

When you're knitting the swatch, it's important to use the same needles you want to knit the garment with—double-pointed needles, straight needles, or a circular, in the same material and from the same manufacturer. Sometimes big surprises await you! The work might be uneven and the stitches and row counts can vary—all because you are using different needles for different materials in different ways.

It can even be good to make a few increases in your gauge swatch to see how the various methods of increasing perform in the actual fabric.

Wash the swatch, lay it out flat without pinning it out and leave it until dry. It might seem excessive, but yarn always behaves somewhat differently after blocking and you want to ensure good results! Some patterns look totally different after washing, and some materials stretch more than others. When you're knitting, you control the yarn; when it's washed, the yarn does what it wants.

Lay the swatch out flat, without stretching it, and measure it with a ruler. It's best to use a transparent plastic ruler that doesn't obscure the knitting so you can see the stitches more clearly. Sometimes it's easier to count the number of stitches and rows on the wrong side.

If the gauge swatch shows that you have too many stitches in 4 in / 10 cm, you should change to larger needles. If you have too few stitches in 4 in / 10 cm, you should change to smaller needles. Sometimes you might need to change the way you hold the needles or the yarn. You can let the yarn lay over your index finger and then in your palm so you can grasp it with your other fingers. If the yarn needs to be held more tightly, you can weave it over your index finger, under the middle finger, over the ring finger, and under the little finger. If the knitting is still too loose, try wrapping the yarn a few times around your little finger.

It's *very* important that your gauge match the given number of stitches and rows in 4 in / 10 cm; otherwise, the garment won't be the right size when it's finished (see photos on pages 28-29). If the numbers don't match, it will also be difficult to fit the sleeves if, for example, you don't know how much each stitch and row extends.

The number of rows in 4 inches / 10 centimeters is not always listed in the instructions. In that case, it's important to note the number of rows from your gauge swatch. In this case, it's important that you have a swatch with the right number of stitches and rows in 4 inches / 10 centimeters as a starting point.

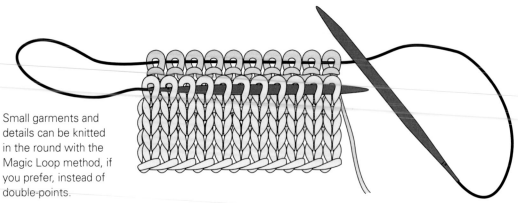

Small garments and details can be knitted in the round with the Magic Loop method, if you prefer, instead of double-points.

Stockinette stitch gauge swatches showing the difference in size of the washed and unwashed silk. Silk spreads out when it's washed.

If you are planning to knit in the round, your gauge swatch should also be knit in the round (and not back and forth) so the stitches will be the same. Use a long circular needle for the so-called "Magic Loop" method: pull out the cord so it's centered between two stitches. The stitches which will be worked next should be on the left needle tip; pull out the right needle tip and cord (see drawing below). Knit the first set of stitches onto the right needle. Now the left needle is empty.

Draw the left needle back to hold the second set of stitches, make a new loop with the cord, and then pull out the right needle. Now you are back to the starting position as shown in the drawing on the previous page. Continue knitting and changing the needle/cord positions.

If you think it's difficult to use the Magic Loop method, you can instead use two double points, knit a row and then slide the stitches back to the starting point without turning the work. Leave a long strand of the yarn floating on the wrong side and then knit a new row. In this way, you can approximate circular knitting and work in stockinette without using any purl stitches. Cut the loose strands on the wrong side and wash the swatch.

If you often knit with the same yarn, it might not be necessary to make a gauge swatch every time, but generally speaking you should try to make it a habit to always knit a gauge swatch. The raw materials and dyes used by yarn companies vary, which can produce different outcomes, and even different skeins of the same brand and type of yarn can vary slightly in thickness or softness and will then behave differently.

Think about ...

✳ Always buy one or two extra skeins of yarn so you'll have plenty for gauge swatches and to have some left over for replacing worn out bands or edges.

✳ If you're changing needle size for stockinette, you also have to change the size for the ribbing and other edges. A rule of thumb is to use needles 1 U.S. / ½-1 mm size smaller for ribbing and edges.

✳ Seed stitch and stockinette will produce different stitch counts with the same yarn and needles. That means that you might need to use different sizes of needle on the same garment. Swatch!

✳ If you are knitting with silk, the yarn might stretch out a lot after blocking, so knit a gauge swatch and wash it!

✳ Never change the knitting techniques in a given pattern without knowing how it will affect the gauge.

✳ For every new piece of knitting, the number of stitches and rows in 4 inches / 10 centimeters is the basis for obtaining good results.

✳ If you want to change the yarn used for a pattern, you must knit a gauge swatch and wash it. Even yarn with the same recommended gauge can vary in all kinds of other ways.

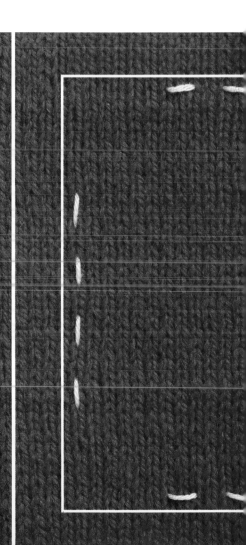

Gauge Swatch

Stockinette stitch.

PHOTO 1 Needles U.S. 2.5 / 3 mm = 26 sts and 39 rows in 4 in / 10 cm

PHOTO 2 Needles U.S. 1.5 / 2.5 mm = 28 sts and 42 rows in 4 in / 10 cm

PHOTO 3 Needles U.S. 4 / 3.5 mm = 24 sts and 38 rows in 4 in / 10 cm

The swatches each have 26 stitches and 39 rows outlined to show what happens when the given gauge is not achieved.

The white square corresponds to 4 x 4 in / 10 x 10 cm in actuality.

1

Dropped or Wrong Stitch

What do you do when you drop a stitch? There are various ways to solve this problem depending on how it happened. If you've lost a stitch and kept knitting for a while before discovering the mistake further down in the piece, I recommend you rip back, because there won't be enough yarn for a new stitch between the existing stitches. You'll get the best results by ripping back all the way to the row with the dropped stitch.

If you've worked a stitch incorrectly or split the yarn, you can generally drop the stitch down to the error and, with the *right side facing you* so you can see what you're doing, pick the stitch up again correctly. A crochet hook of the right size can be used to latch the stitch back up and make this tricky process easier. Check the wrong side and make sure you've caught up all the strands and rows and picked up the strands in the right order, and that the stitches are not twisted. Hold the knitting up to a light source to make it easier to see.

If the picked-up stitch makes a visible vertical line in your knitting, it might be better to rip back and reknit. With some yarns, it's difficult to eliminate that type of unevenness even after blocking.

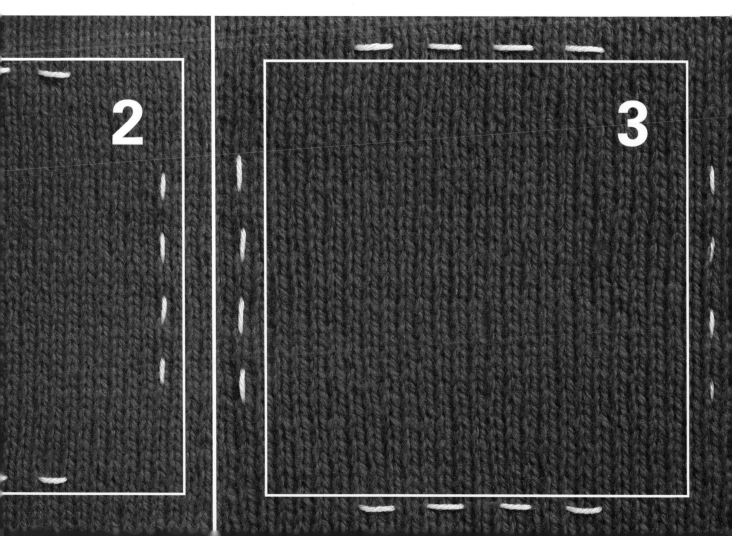

Markers

MARKING ROWS

In your knitting, you should always count the rows so each of the pieces will be the same length. You may not always be in the same mood each time you are knitting and that will show! If you measure with a measuring tape, you'll get a different result each time. Measuring tapes can be used to quickly check, for example, the length and width of the various parts.

To make it easier to count rows, you can take a length of contrast color cotton yarn and weave it through the knitting all the way from the bottom to the top. Weave it in between two stitches, on, say, every fifth row or for every increase/decrease row—alternating on

The white marking thread on the front shows the increases on the side as well as the binding off for the armholes and neckline. The red marking thread on the body and sleeve indicate the number of repeats in the respective directions for fitting the sleeve stitches against the rows on the body—two stitches for every three rows.

the right and wrong sides. Insert the yarn under the row that applies to the marking. You can mark the front and back pieces as well as the sleeves this way.

The cotton yarn should begin below the first row a little in from the side and remain in the knitting until the finishing is completely done.

MARKING THE BIND-OFFS

You can also use cotton yarn to mark where you have bound off for the armholes and neck shaping as well as the rows between buttonholes and the number of rows in vertical buttonholes.

To mark an armhole, lay the yarn in on the same row as for the binding off, knit a few stitches and then bring the yarn through between two new stitches on the same row. That way, you'll have a clear and distinct marking that will be easy to follow.

You can easily develop your own marking system. The way you do it doesn't really matter, only that you use the same method throughout so you'll always know what the markings mean. At first, it might be a little difficult to figure out a way that works for you, but over time a marking system will be worth its weight in gold, so don't give up!

Marking with yarn will be very useful when you, for example, sew the side seams. With markings to guide you, you can make sure the increases and decreases align. In addition, if you know how many stitches and rows are in 4 inches / 10 centimeters, you don't really need to measure the work as long as you're using the thread markers—provided, of course, that you knitted a gauge swatch. It couldn't be easier or neater.

MARKING THE NUMBER OF STITCHES

When casting on several hundred stitches, it's necessary to mark, for example, every 50th stitch. The easiest and cheapest method is to knot a little ring of mercerized cotton yarn and slide it onto the needle after a given number of stitches. You can also use small rubber bands or plastic ring markers (available in several sizes). In principle, you can use whatever kind of marker you want, but make sure you don't use anything sharp that could damage the knitting.

Casting On

There are many methods for casting on stitches. The most common is probably the long-tail method, but there are many other alternatives, such as the useful and sturdy cable cast-on.

I think the garment should determine what type of cast-on to use as well as the knitted lower edge of the body, sleeves, and neckband. What type of garment are you knitting? Will it be practical or fine? What knitting technique will you use? Does the garment need a more elastic cast-on or a firmer edge? Try out a few methods and see which one is best for the garment you want to knit. Make a little swatch of the cast-on and the bind-off method you've chosen. See how they match up with each other and with the garment in the chosen yarn.

Some cast-on and bind-off methods tend to be a little bulky—so use a thinner needle. Some methods are tighter—you may want to use a slightly larger needle. Don't forget to block your gauge swatch.

For all the cast-on methods, add a little extra length of yarn when calculating the yarn amount. This way, you'll have some yarn ready for the side seams. Always cast on over one needle. The abbreviation for "cast on" is "CO".

LONG-TAIL CAST-ON

This method for casting on makes a relatively firm, flexible, and strong edge. Estimate four times the width of the finished piece for the length needed for the loose end.

Cast the stitches onto *one* needle, using the same size as for the edge of the garment.

WORK AS FOLLOWS • Make a slip knot loop and place it on the right needle. Hold the loose end of the yarn over your left thumb and the other strand (from the yarn ball) over your left index finger—from the inside and outwards—and, *at the same time*, grasp both ends in your left hand.

Insert the right needle under the front strand over your thumb, up over the next strand and then catch the strand looped around your index finger. Use the right needle to bring the strand/stitch back through the loop around the thumb, drop the loop and tighten the yarn. Repeat from * to *.

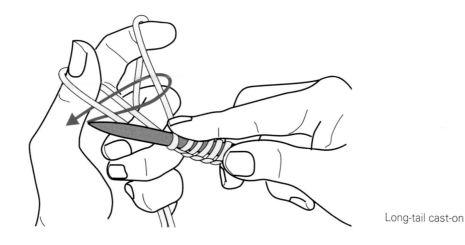

Long-tail cast-on

- The smooth edge formed by the cast-on is the right side of the fabric. The first row is always a wrong side row when you are working back and forth.
- The long-tail cast-on is suitable for all types of knitting: garter stitch, stockinette, ribbing, etc.
- The long-tail cast-on also matches the standard bind-off method well.

LONG-TAIL CAST-ON WITH DOUBLED YARN OVER THE THUMB

If you need a more elastic edge, as, for example, on a sock leg, you can try doubling the strand over the thumb while using a single strand over your index finger. The loose thumb strand should be about eight times the width of the finished piece. Double the strand and hold it over your thumb. This makes a sturdier and stronger cast-on than the regular long-tail method.

WORK AS FOLLOWS • Work as for the regular long-tail cast-on over *one* needle. Pull the strands so they will be even and the edge smooth and fine.

Think about …

… when you use the long-tail cast-on method, never cast on over two needles! This makes a row of long, unattractive stitches with large loops that won't in any way contribute to a more elastic edge, although that's often cited as the purpose. It's the strand over the thumb that determines how elastic the cast-on will be, not doubled needles.

- The right side of the cast-on faces you and can be considered the first row on the right side.
- This cast-on method is bulkier than the regular method and can be combined with a bind-off worked over two rows.

An alternative for a more flexible cast-on is to cast on two stitches with long-tail and then pass the first stitch over the second—one stitch now remains on the right needle. Cast on two new stitches and pass the first stitch over the second. Two stitches are now on the right needle. Continue casting on two stitches and passing the first over the second until you have the desired number of stitches.

DOUBLE LONG-TAIL CAST-ON

This method is worked as for regular long-tail. Estimate four times the finished fabric width for the loose (thumb) end. Use one needle, the same size as for the edge of the knitting. This method has many names, including "German twisted cast-on" and "old Norwegian cast-on."

WORK AS FOLLOWS • Make a slip knot and place it over the right needle. Arrange the yarn over the thumb and index finger as for regular long-tail.

   * Insert the right needle under both strands on the thumb, catch the inner strand on thumb and bring the needle with the yarn forward, under the front strand on the thumb, and then up to the strand on the index finger (1). Catch the front strand on the index finger (2) and bring the strand towards the thumb and down through the loop (3) that

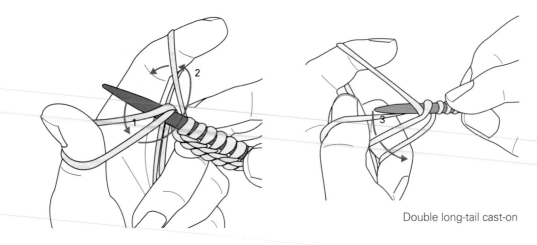

Double long-tail cast-on

was formed around the thumb on Step 1. Release the loop and tighten the stitch*. Repeat * to *.

- The right side faces you as you cast on, so, the first row will always be on the wrong side when working
- The double long-tail cast-on can be paired with a twisted bind-off.

KNITTED CAST-ON

This type of cast-on is worked with two needles precisely as for regular knitting. The stitches are formed with the yarn coming from the ball. The result is a reversible, very loose, elastic, but not especially stable cast-on edge.

The knitted cast-on can be used as a decorative edge on scarves or cuffs with lace patterns and on children's clothing. It's not suitable for hard-wearing garments.

WORK AS FOLLOWS • Make a slip knot loop and place it on the left needle. *Insert the right needle into the loop and catch the working yarn—this makes a new stitch on the right needle. Now move the new stitch to the left needle and tighten the yarn*. Repeat * to *. When you move the stitch to the left needle, it should make a half turn clockwise: insert the left needle into the front loop from right to left, into the stitch as it sits on the right needle.

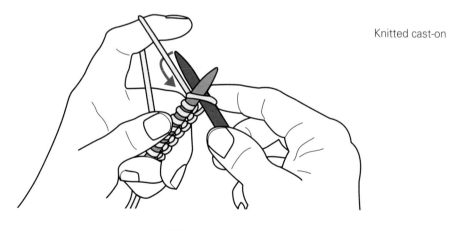

Knitted cast-on

Think about ...

... knit the first row with twisted knit stitches. This provides a firmer edge than one knitted with untwisted stitches.

CABLE CAST-ON

This is a fantastic cast-on method that can be used for pretty much every garment and it's especially good for ribbing and garter stitch. The cable cast-on is sturdy and strong but also fairly elastic. Another advantage is that if you've cast on too many stitches, you only have to slide the left needle out and pull the yarn to make the extra stitches disappear. The stitches are formed by the strand coming from the ball.

WORK AS FOLLOWS • Make a slip knot loop and place it on the left needle. Make another stitch as for the knitted cast-on (see previous page) and move the stitch to the left needle.

*Insert the right needle, front to back, *between* the outermost two stitches on the left needle—in other words, behind the newest stitch. Catch the yarn with the right needle to make a new stitch, remove the needle with the new stitch and move it to the left needle, twisting the stitch a half turn clockwise as it's placed on the needle*. Repeat * to *.

• The right side of this cast-on faces you as you cast on so the first row will be knitted on the right side as you work back and forth.
• This method goes well with a one-over-two bind-off.

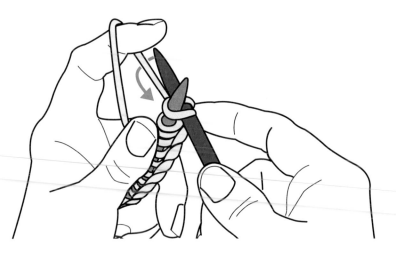

Cable cast-on

SIMPLE LOOP CAST-ON

The loop cast-on is *not* suitable for lower edges on garments; it's used for casting on new stitches at the side of the front and back pieces when knitting a sweater from cuff to cuff. You can also use this cast-on to add stitches at the underside of a sleeve that will be knitted in one piece with the body, the so-called penguin sleeve. The sides are joined by grafting and the cast-on edge stays free.

In both these circumstances, the loop cast-on can be substituted with a provisional cast-on (for example, a crocheted cord, see page 39). The various parts are then joined by grafting.

WORK AS FOLLOWS • In your right hand, hold the yarn at the same time as making the first stitches or make a slip knot loop which you can remove later. The yarn which forms the stitches comes directly from the ball.

Hold the needle in the right hand and the yarn in the left. *Lay the yarn over the thumb so that the yarn loops on the front of the thumb, that is, the side facing you. Insert the needle front to back, under the front strand, slip the loop off the thumb, and tighten the stitch that has formed on the needle*. Repeat * to *.

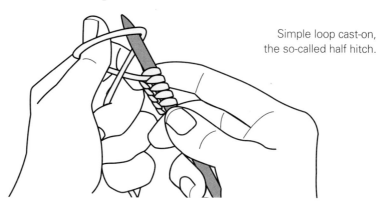

Simple loop cast-on, the so-called half hitch.

Think about ...

... if you are going to cast on in stages, you can make a smoother transition between the steps by slipping the first stitch when you knit the first row after the cast-on. When you get back to the same place in the knitting, and want to cast on new stitches, knit the slipped stitch of the previous row before casting on the next set of stitches. (See the photo at bottom left on page 49).

Turn and begin knitting from the right side. Slip the first stitch, knit the remaining stitches through the *back* loop so that the cast-on edge will be loose and flexible and won't take up any space when you want to sew a side seam. If you work the first row as usual, through the front loops, the cast-on will be somewhat sturdier.

The stitches in this cast-on are the same type of loop (also called a half hitch) used for securing the knitting at the end of the row before you put the knitting aside (see page 12).

CHANNEL ISLAND CAST-ON

This cast-on forms an unusual and pretty edge because it's shaped by two different types of stitches, a knot stitch and a yarnover. It is excellent for k1, p1 ribbing. If you later want to have an especially nice finish to match this cast-on, you can crochet crab stitch (single crochet worked backwards).

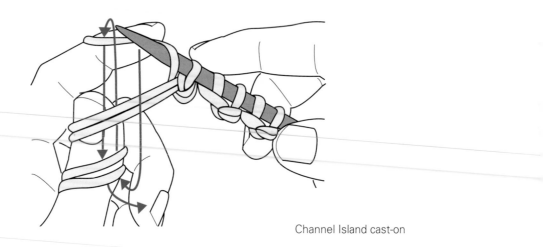

Channel Island cast-on

WORK AS FOLLOWS • Prepare a doubled strand and a single strand of yarn. Estimate the doubled yarn as four times the length of the knitting and the single strand comes directly from the ball. Make a slip knot loop with all the strands. (Once you've learned the technique well, you can skip the slip knot; it's only used to help get you started and will be removed once you start knitting.)

Wrap the doubled yarn once around your thumb so the doubled strands that will encircle each stitch lie on the top/front of the thumb. The single strand lies over the index finger as for the long-tail cast-on. The strands are held together in the left hand. Make a yarnover on the needle with the single strand. Next, insert the needle under the strands wrapped around your thumb and catch the strand from the index finger. Release the strands from the thumb and tighten stitch. Rep * to *.

- The right side will face you as you cast on so you'll begin working on the wrong side if you are working back and forth.
- This cast-on pairs well with a crocheted bind-off with single crochet back and forth.

Think about …

✳ The knot stitch is worked as a knit stitch and the yarnover as a purl stitch as seen from the right side in a k1, p1 rib.

✳ If you are using this cast-on for circular knitting, you have to be careful when you join the stitches into a ring so that they match. That is to say, a knot stitch should be next to a yarnover and not next to another knot stitch.

CROCHET CHAIN CAST-ON

This cast-on method is the basis for a folded edge that can either be sewn down with duplicate stitch afterwards or knitted together as you work. Use a crochet hook that corresponds in size to your knitting needles.

WORK AS FOLLOWS • Using 8/4 mercerized cotton, make a crochet chain a little longer than needed for the cast-on. Fasten off yarn. Be careful not to work the chain stitches too tightly.

Turn the cord, hold it in your left hand with the right side down along your middle finger, and pick up stitches through the little stitch loop on the underside of the cord which now faces upwards. Use a knitting needle and the yarn you'll be knitting with. Pick up

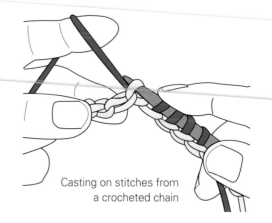

Casting on stitches from a crocheted chain

several more stitches than needed and let the first stitches you cast on stay *unworked* on the needle for a few rows. In this way, the outermost stitches at the beginning of the first row will be more even.

If you find it hard to crochet, you can cast on the exact number of stitches with cotton yarn and then knit a few rows. These rows will be removed later on, just as with a crocheted chain. You might need some scissors to help remove the cotton yarn.

TWO-STEP CAST-ON

This cast-on is worked in two steps and is excellent for k1, p1 ribbing. First cast on half the total number of stitches needed from a crocheted chain and after a few rows of stockinette, remove the crocheted chain and pick up the remaining stitches. This results in a narrow round edge that is nice in combination with a bind-off sewn with Kitchener stitch after you've worked a few rows in double knitting (see photo page 49). This cast-on might not work well for a hard-wearing garment but it will look nice!

You'll always have an odd number of stitches when you cast on this way.

WORK AS FOLLOWS • Crochet a chain using mercerized cotton yarn; chaining half the number of stitches needed. Do not chain too hard. Turn the chain, hold it in your left hand with the right side along your middle finger and pick up *half* the total stitch count through the small loops on the underside of the chain which now faces upwards (see drawing

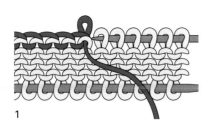

1

Two-step cast-on. After a few rows in stockinette, remove the cotton yarn and place the released stitches on a knitting needle.

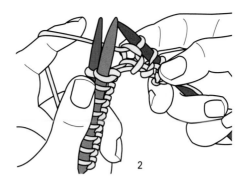

2

Now alternately purl 1 stitch from the back needle and knit 1 from the front needle to double the stitch count.

above). Use a knitting needle or crochet hook and the yarn you'll knit with. **NOTE**: Pick up a few extra stitches that you *won't* actually knit but which will remain on the needles for a few rows—the first cast-on stitches will be neater and more even this way.

Work in stockinette for a total of three rows, with the first row purled on the wrong side. Now there are four rows including the cast-on row. If you want a more conspicuous edge, you can work four rows, beginning with a knit row. In that case, you'll have five rows total, including the cast-on row. The *last* stockinette row is *always* worked on the wrong side.

Now remove the crochet chain and, *at the same time*, place the released stitches (the loops from the cast-on row) on a smaller needle (1). There will be one stitch less on the needle when the chain cord is removed.

Turn the stockinette section, with wrong side facing wrong side and the front facing you—knit 1 edge stitch from the front needle, *purl 1 from the back needle, knit 1 from the front needle* (2). Repeat * to * across and end with purl 1, and then knit 1 edge stitch from the front needle. Continue in k1, p1 ribbing.

• This cast-on pairs well with a sewn bind-off.

> **Think about ...**
> ✳ When you cast on stitches for a garment, you should consider how well it works with the pattern at the side and the edge stitches.
> ✳ It can be simpler to cast on and work around on a circular. In that case, you need an even number of stitches so increase one stitch at an appropriate place.

After completing the cast-on, divide the work into two sections—front and back—and work in ribbing. Consider how to match the pattern and add an edge stitch at each side of the pieces so you'll have them to use for seaming the sides later on.

You can also work the ribbing on a circular (even if ribbing is usually worked back and forth—see page 60) and then divide the work into front and back pieces. Don't forget to add an edge stitch at each side.

MY VARIATION ON THE LONG-TAIL CAST-ON WITH TWO COLORS

This cast-on is firm and decorative. It's very nice for cuffs that are knitted with a texture pattern or firm two-color knitting. To match it, use the standard bind-off method with two colors.

The cast-on can be the base for a stockinette edge with two colors, alternating colors, and then the main color continues up nicely into single color stockinette. You can even work garter stitch—knitting on both right and wrong sides—on the stitch worked with the contrast color. The main color stitches continue in stockinette and, in that way, you'll have a nice effect on the edge below.

If you are working in k1, p1 ribbing where the contrast color is used for the vertical purl line, it won't really be ribbing with ribbing's characteristics. In that case, it would be easier to knit the edge on a circular (ribbing is usually worked back and forth, see page 60).

Hold the yarn the same way throughout the edge—see two-color knitting on page 133.

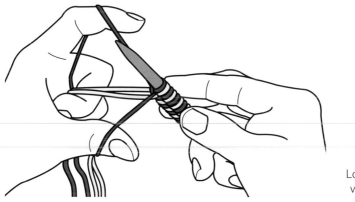

Long-tail cast-on
with two colors

WORK AS FOLLOWS • Use two colors. Estimate four times the finished width for the loose strand of each color. Make a slip knot loop, first one with the main color and then another with the contrast color. Place both loops on the right needle as for regular long-tail cast-on. Lay the main color strands in the middle and the contrast color strands outermost at each side.

*Grasp the main color strands as for regular long-tail cast-on and make a stitch. Change the color pairs: while still holding the contrast color strands, use your middle finger to catch the contrast color strands *between* the two other strands. Release the main color strands and let them hang out, one strand to each side. Make a new stitch with the main color following the same steps as for regular long-tail cast-on. Change colors*. Rep * to *.

- The right side faces you while casting on so the first row will be worked on the wrong side when knitting back and forth.
- Try this method with only one color but with two pairs of strands as above. This forms a nice, strong edge.
- You can combine this cast-on with a standard bind-off in two colors.

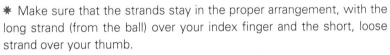

Think about ...

＊ Make sure that the strands stay in the proper arrangement, with the long strand (from the ball) over your index finger and the short, loose strand over your thumb.

＊ Don't forget to tighten the strands after each stitch so the pattern forms evenly.

＊ It takes a little patience to work this cast-on and you need to practice before casting on for a whole garment.

TWO-COLOR KNITTED CAST-ON

This cast-on is formed by using two different colors on the cast-on row and makes a decorative band on the lower edge of the garment. It's also called the "crocheted" cast-on. It looks good with an edge worked in a texture pattern.

At first this cast-on method can be difficult to get even and nice, so practice.

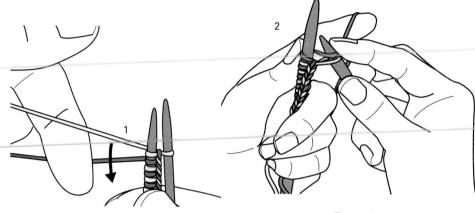

Two-color knitted cast-on

WORK AS FOLLOWS • Make a slip knot loop with each color and place the dark yarn on the left needle and the light yarn on the right needle. Hold a needle in each hand. The strands are held in the left hand on the wrong side of the piece.

* Lay the light strand over the dark one (1). Take the dark strand and lay it clockwise over the left needle (2). Use the right needle to catch the same strand and bring it through the stitch on the right needle. Now there's a dark stitch on the left needle. Lay the dark strand over the light on on the wrong side of the piece and follow the same steps to make a light stitch on the left needle*. Repeat * to *.

Tighten the strands so that the stitches on the left needle are even and the chain along the cast-on edge on the right side is nice and even. When you've cast on the number of stitches required, you can remove the first stitches.

• Choose the side away from you when casting-on as the right side.
• When binding off a garment with this cast-on, try a reversible bind-off with two colors.

Think about ...

✳ You can use a crochet hook to help catch the strand and draw it through the stitch instead of using the right needle.

✳ Tighten the strands after every new stitch and make sure the edge is nice and even.

✳ Make sure that the cast-on stitches match when joining the sides.

Binding Off

Binding off a garment means that the stitches that won't be used any more will be secured in a neat and flexible way on a knitted row. In general, binding off is worked on the right side. There are various types of bind-off methods, some are stronger than others while some are like small jewels that are purely decorative. When binding off, choose a method that matches the knitting and the function.

The shoulders on the back and the straight part of the neckline on the front and back are bound off twice when extra support is desired. If you want more flexible shoulders and a softer neckline you can place the stitches on a holder (or bind them off with cotton yarn that will be removed later) and use these live stitches when finishing the garment. You can also bind off on a sleeve or on a pullover that is worked down from the neckline. A drop shoulder sleeve that is worked up from the cuff is not bound off but attached to the armhole with Kitchener stitch.

It's always important that the bind-off maintains the same tension as for the knitting after being blocked. If you think that it's hard to keep an even tension, try a different size needle (either smaller or larger) for the bind-off row. You need to test various options because the result depends on which type of bind-off you choose. In some cases, the needle must be much smaller and in other cases you need to try a much bigger needle.

There are many different methods for binding off knitting. The easiest and the most common is worked by first knitting two stitches and then passing the first stitch over the second. Continue the same way, knit a new stitch, pass the previous stitch over the new stitch, etc. This bind-off is referred to as the standard bind-off but has several other names including the lift-off or chain bind-off. This is the basic bind-off you would use for a shoulder or when binding off at the center of the front or back of a neckline.

STANDARD BIND-OFF

The standard bind-off is elastic and flexible and can be used for all kinds of knitting and is the most common style of binding off. With this method as the base, you can bind off in many fine ways. In texts, this is abbreviated as BO (also termed casting off, in British knitting). You can use this bind-off on both right and wrong sides—just follow the same knitting technique as in your project—knit stitch over knit and purl over purl.

The bind-off edge might bias a little if you are working in stockinette or bind off in ribbing. The chain of stitches might also point in different directions depending on which side you have chosen to bind off on.

The bind-off row should have the same tension as for the knitting after blocking, which means that you might need to use a larger needle. If the last stitch on the edge (the edge stitch) tends to be a little loose, you can work it together with the edge stitch on the row below before you pass the last stitch over.

If you are binding off in circular knitting with the standard method, when you get to the end of the round, insert the needle once again into the very first stitch and pass the last one over. This join will look especially neat.

WORK AS FOLLOWS • Work two stitches, pass the first one over the second, *work a new stitch and pass the previous one over it*. Repeat * to *.

If you are knitting a shawl and want the bind-off to be secure but also flexible, work one stitch, *yarnover onto the right needle, work the outermost stitch on the left needle and pass the stitch and yarnover on the right needle over the last worked stitch*. Repeat * to *.

• The standard bind-off pairs well with the long-tail cast-on.

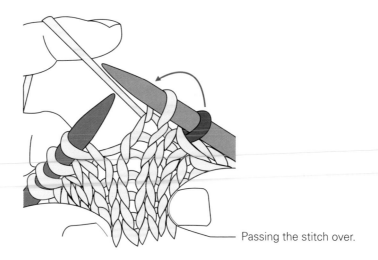

Passing the stitch over.

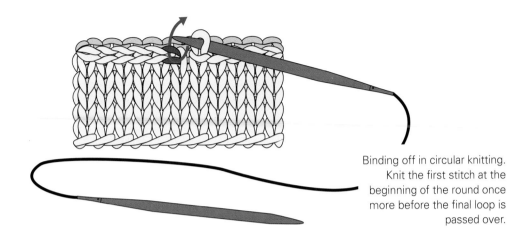

Binding off in circular knitting. Knit the first stitch at the beginning of the round once more before the final loop is passed over.

STANDARD BIND-OFF WITH TWO COLORS

If you cast on or worked the neckband with two colors, alternating the colors, it would look good to also bind off with two colors. The two-color bind-off can also make a pleasing effect on a single color, ribbed neckband.

By using two colors for the standard bind-off, you can match the patterning on the bind-off edge with the cast-on edge and the stitches on each will face the same direction.

The bind-off can be worked on either the right or wrong side and your choice will determine which direction the chain will face. Binding off on the *wrong side* is worked with *purl stitches* alternating in the contrast and main colors. Binding off on *the right side* is the same but worked with *knit* stitches. **NOTE**: Make sure that the colors in the bind-off match those in the cast-on. This is especially important for a small piece, as for example, a cuff where the eye can follow the stitch lines. The color not in use is always stranded on the wrong side.

WORK AS FOLLOWS • Use two colors, a main color and a contrast color. Hold the strands as for two-color stranded knitting and begin by mak-ing a stitch of each color. Pass the first stitch over the second. *Make a new stitch with the next color in turn and pass the previous stitch over the second one*. Repeat * to *. Make sure that the stitches are all the same size.

For ribbing, follow the sequence of stitches as established. Don't forget to strand the color not in use on the wrong side of the piece.

• This bind-off matches a long-tail cast-on with two colors.

Long-tail cast-on—compare what happens to the cast-on edge with single and doubled needles. **TOP PHOTO** Long-tail cast-on over doubled needles. Stockinette stitch. Standard bind-off. **BOTTOM PHOTO** Long-tail cast-on over single needle. Stockinette stitch. Standard bind-off.

TOP PHOTO Simple loop cast-on; the first row is knitted. Standard bind-off. **BOTTOM PHOTO** Simple loop cast-on; the first row is worked in twisted knit. Standard bind-off.

Double long-tail cast-on. K1, p1 ribbing. Twisted bind-off.

Long-tail cast-on with doubled strand over thumb. K1, p1 ribbing. Bind-off worked over two rows.

Knitted cast-on with two colors. **TOP PHOTO** Stockinette stitch. Reversible bind-off on the right side with two colors. **BOTTOM PHOTO** Texture stitch. Reversible bind-off with two colors. The bind-off was made in reverse (step one on the wrong side so the stitches face the same direction on the

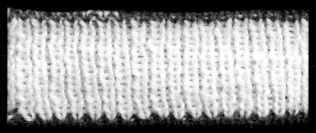

My variation of the long-tail cast-on worked on the wrong side with the two-colors bind-off. **TOP PHOTO** Stockinette stitch with the main color dominant.
BOTTOM PHOTO Stockinette stitch with the main color in one stitch line and the contrast color in garter stitch on alternating stitch lines.

Channel Island cast-on. **TOP PHOTO** K1, p1 ribbing, finished with two rows of crochet, one row of single crochet in each direction. **BOTTOM PHOTO** K1, p1 ribbing, finished with a row of crab stitch (single crochet worked backwards).

Cast-on from a crocheted chain. Stockinette.

Two-step cast-on, four rows stockinette including the cast-on row. K1, p1 ribbing. Bind-off with double knitting and sewn bind-off.

Easy cast-on in three steps. Stockinette.
An example of how the stitches can be increased at the side when, for example, the sweater is worked from sleeve to sleeve.

Cable cast-on. Stockinette. One over two bind-off.

ONE-OVER-TWO BIND-OFF

With this one-over-two or decrease bind-off, you'll have an impressive, somewhat tight, and distinct finishing that is also strong.

WORK AS FOLLOWS • K3, pass the first knitted stitch over the other two. *K1 and pass the outermost stitch from the right over the other two stitches*. Repeat * to *. At the end, when two stitches remain, make a standard one-over-one bind-off. Cut yarn and bring end through the stitch.

- To make it extra fun—use three colors, one stitch in each color.
- The bind-off row has a tendency to pull together so use a larger needle. Test to find what size works best for your knitting.
- This bind-off pairs well with the cable cast-on.

BIND-OFF OVER TWO ROWS

This bind-off method can be used to finish k1, p1 ribbing.

WORK AS FOLLOWS • *Work k1, p1 and and pass the knit stitch over the purl stitch*. Repeat * to *. Half of the stitch count remains.

Cut yarn and turn work. Pass the first stitch over the second. Continue passing one stitch over the next one until only one stitch remains. The principle is the same as for standard bind-off but without knitting the stitches. It's easier to work with a crochet hook. Fasten off the last stitch.

- This bind-off tends to pull together so use a larger needle.
- Pair this bind-off with the double long-tail cast-on.

TWISTED BIND-OFF

The twisted bind-off makes a somewhat firmer finishing and can be used, for example, for toe-up socks with the leg bound off at the top, sleeves that are worked from the top down as well as neckbands on heavier, larger outer garments.

This bind-off makes a nice chain edge that, in some cases, looks like standard bind-off but it's firmer due to the twisted stitches. If you want

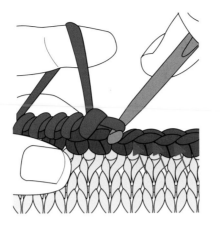

Twisted bind-off

to have a noticeable bind-off to finish a ribbed neckband, you can use this method because it falls towards the right side with the fine chain edge visible.

WORK AS FOLLOWS • Knit one stitch. *Slip the stitch back to the left needle and knit the first two stitches together through back loops*. Repeat * to *.

You can produce a somewhat different chain effect on the bind-off edge if you twist the stitch as you slip it back to the left needle. That is, move the stitch to the left needle by twisting it a half turn, taking it from the front when you move it off the right needle. Try it—it's cool!

The bind-off row should be the same tension as the overall knitting after blocking, so sample to make sure you use the right needle size.

• This pairs well with the double long-tail cast-on.

CROCHETED BIND-OFF WITH SINGLE CROCHET

This method of binding off produces a pretty beaded edge that is very firm and is a good finish on a neckband, for example. It's strong and can be redone if it happens to rip.

WORK AS FOLLOWS • Bind off with the standard bind-off method. On a circularly-knitted neckband, do not cut the yarn you knitted with but use it for the crocheted bind-off.

Use a crochet hook in the same size as the knitting needle used for

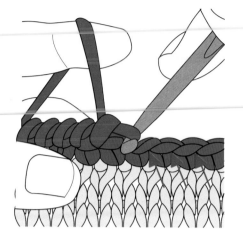

the band. With right side facing, work a row of single crochet. Insert the hook directly under the bind-off row, through both loops. Make a chain stitch at the end of the row but *do not turn*. Working *backwards*, work a row of crab stitch (single crochet worked from left to right). Work firmly but make sure the edge is still flexible.

If you think that the edge is too clumsy, try omitting the first row of single crochet. Begin the crab stitch from left to right and insert the hook under the bind-off row as described above. Crocheting backwards takes a little patience at first but don't give up!

• This bind-off method pairs well with the Channel Islands cast-on.

SEWN BIND-OFF

This bind-off method is used for k1, p1 ribbing. Work with the right side facing. Estimate a length of yarn four times the width of the finished piece, around, for example, the neckband, plus a little extra.

Binding off with Kitchener Stitch
Sew with the right side facing. Insert the needle through the back of the first (knit) stitch on the needle and then from the back through the second stitch (purl). Bring the yarn through and drop the stitches from the needle. (If you knitted in the round, you do not need to do these first two preparatory stitches but can begin directly with the instructions below.)

*Insert the needle from the front into the knit stitch (1), past the

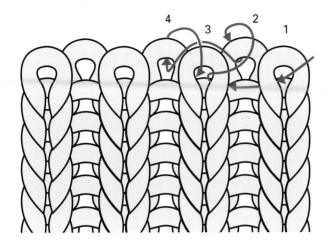

Binding off with
Kitchener stitch

purl stitch (2) and in through the back of the knit stitch (3)—the stitch that now sits outermost on the left needle. Bring the yarn through and drop the stitch.

Insert the needle from the back through the purl stitch (2), past the knit stitch (3) and into the front of the purl stitch (4), which now sits outermost on the left needle. Bring yarn through*.

Repeat * to * (don't worry about the numbers in parentheses which are just there to help with the first few stitches).

When you bring out the yarn from each stitch, make sure it matches the tension of the knitting as the bind-off corresponds to a knitted row.

Tips for maintaining the sequence of steps through the stitches
Kitchener stitch for the sewn bind-off is made exactly the same way as when two pieces of stockinette knitting are joined, as for a shoulder seam. Think of the purl stitches as equivalent to those on the back needle and the knit stitches as those on the front needle.

Alternately, you can move all the purl stitches to another needle or a strand of yarn and keep the knit stitches on a second needle and then work the Kitchener stitch join as if for a shoulder seam with live stitches. You can also try holding a length of contrast color sewing thread with the yarn you are sewing with. The sewing thread can be removed later but it will help you see the stitches better as you work.

• This bind-off pairs well with the two-step cast-on.

SEWN BIND-OFF FOR DOUBLE KNITTING

For a softer rounding before the sewn bind-off row—corresponding to the edge from a two-step cast-on—the last row can be substituted with two rows of double knitting, with one row in each "layer"—one on the right side and one on the wrong side. It's easiest to work with an even number of stitches but not necessary when you are working back and forth.

WORK AS FOLLOWS • On the right side: *Knit the knit stitch, slip the purl stitch purlwise with yarn *in front**. Repeat * to *. Work the next row the same way, so that the stitch which was previously slipped is now knit and the stitch you knitted is now slipped purlwise with yarn in front.

If you are working around on a neckband, on the second round, purl the previously slipped stitch and slip the knitted stitch purlwise with yarn *behind*. **NOTE**: In that case, make sure that you have an even number of stitches.

REVERSIBLE BIND-OFF

This method of binding off makes an edge that is alike on both sides. If you use an accent color, the bind-off will make a lovely embellishment

WORK AS FOLLOWS • *Step 1, on the right side: Knit 1, purl 2 together; turn. Step 2, on the wrong side: Slip 1 stitch knitwise with the yarn behind, slip 1 stitch purlwise with yarn in front; turn*. Repeat * to *, each time decreasing by 1 stitch.

Use a smaller needle for this bind-off row. Try out various needles to see what works best for the yarn you are using.

This type of bind-off can be worked on both sides and that means that the stitches' chain will point in different directions.

If you want to use two colors, hold the strands as usual in your left hand. The strand that you used last lies *over* the "waiting" strand from left to right. Tighten the strands so the stitches are equal sized. Use one color for each repeat round. When are you comfortable with the technique you can catch the stitches in Step 2 without turning the work.

• This bind-off matches the two-color knitted cast-on.

Edge Stitches

The little edge stitch has a large and important role in knitting. It can be worked in many different ways depending on how the garment will be sewn together, how the stitches and rows relate to each other, or if the stitches are visible as, for example, on a front edge.

In general, we can say that edge stitches are not worked to widen the edge or side and they also should not be too tight.

Edge stitches are always worked on *every* row on a garment that will be joined at the sides, when a sleeve will be sewn in, when a button band will be sewn to a front edge, or when stitches will be picked up along a knitted edge. This applies no matter what's stated in your instructions!

The only exception is for techniques in which two rows do not rise as much in length as two knitted edge stitches. That can be a technique where every other stitch is worked and the alternate stitches are slipped on every row. "Bird's feet" (similar to honeycomb) and various slip stitch patterns are examples of techniques where the side will be bulky if the edge stitch is worked on every row.

An excellent edge stitch in stockinette and ribbing is purled at the beginning of the row and worked as a twisted knit at the end of the row. The edge stitches will be firm and produce a pleasing effect on the wrong side of the side seam. Tighten a little extra at the side and on the yarn when you work the stitch.

For a garter-stitch garment which will be sewn together, the edge stitch is *always* knitted at both the beginning and end of every row to make an edge that will be neat and flexible for sewing up the side. The variation described above for stockinette, where the edge stitch is purled at the beginning of the row and knitted through the back loop at the end of the row, would make a bulky edge in garter stitch. Garter edge stitches at both the beginning and end of every row also work excellently for stockinette, particularly if you have difficulty keeping the edge even with twisted knit stitches. In stockinette/ribbing, you can also work the edge stitch to match the pattern at the beginning and end of every row. Knit on the right side and purl on the wrong side. Try the options to see which you like best.

For seed stitch, work the edge stitch on every row to follow the pat-

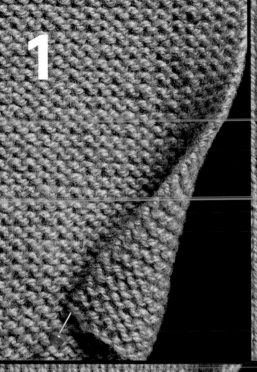

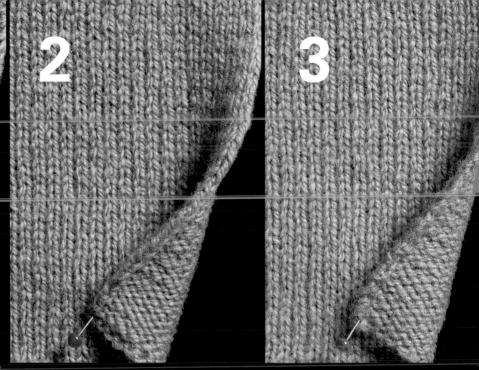

Edge stitches joined at the sides

PHOTO 1 Garter stitch. First and last stitch knitted on every row.

PHOTO 2 Stockinette. First stitch purled, last stitch knit through back loop.

PHOTO 3 Stockinette. Edge stitch knit at the beginning and end of every row.

PHOTO 4 Stockinette. Edge stitch worked to match the pattern at the beginning and end of every row.

PHOTO 5 K1, p1 ribbing. First stitch is purled, and the last stitch knit through back loop on every row.

PHOTO 6 Seed stitch. Edge stitch worked at beginning and end of every to match patterning.

PHOTO 7 "Bird's Feet." Slip first stitch purlwise with yarn in front, knit last stitch. The edge stitches are worked on alternate rows to match the gauge of the knitting.

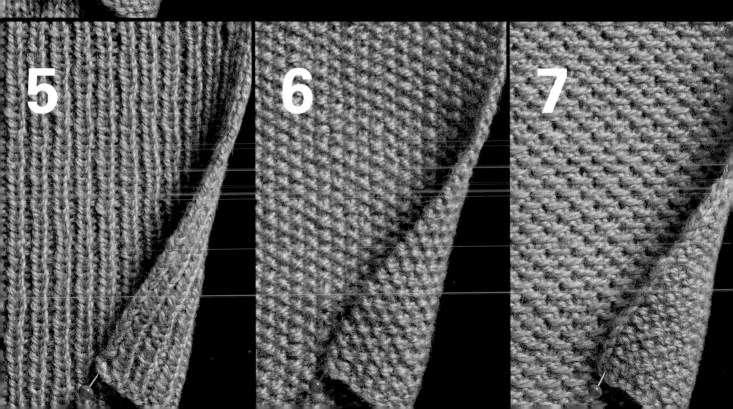

terning. Knit at the beginning of the row and purl at the end of the row and the seams will look good.

EDGE STITCHES THAT WON'T BE JOINED AT THE SIDES

Slipped edge stitches, or so-called chain stitches, are used on garment pieces that won't be sewn together, such as front edges, button/button-hole bands on cardigans, and along the long sides of scarves and shawls. Chain edges can be a decorative element in an otherwise simple fabric or create a distinctive edge.

Slipped stitches can be made and combined in various ways so that the front edges will look good and function, in some cases, as a foldline. This is the same for all techniques, whether ribbing, garter stitch, or stockinette.

In a garter stitch piece, you'll produce a nice edge if you slip the last two stitches purlwise with yarn in front and knit them at the beginning of the row. Alternatively, you can try slipping the stitches at the beginning of the row and working them at the end, or slipping the stitches at the beginning *and* end on one side and working them on the other side. The look will vary a little bit depending on whether you want to have them more reversible as on, for example, a scarf or the front edges of a cardigan. Sample to see what you like.

Another good edging for garter-stitch cardigans or garter-stitch front bands is this one: on the right side, slip the next-to-last outermost stitch purlwise with yarn on wrong side of work and purl it on the wrong side. The outermost stitch is knit on *every* row.

If you are working in stockinette on a piece that won't be sewn together, as for a scarf, you can try a chain edge stitch outermost on each edge or choose another combination that will stabilize the edge. Your choice depends somewhat on the quality of the knitting..

Edge stitches as a foldline

If you are working a ribbed button band or scarf, you might want to sample various types of foldline stitch. A foldline stitch is slipped purlwise on the right side, with yarn behind and purled on the wrong side.

In a k1, p1 ribbing, the foldline stitch lies at the outer edge as in the example below. This edge is nice with the two-step cast-on and a sewn bind-off.

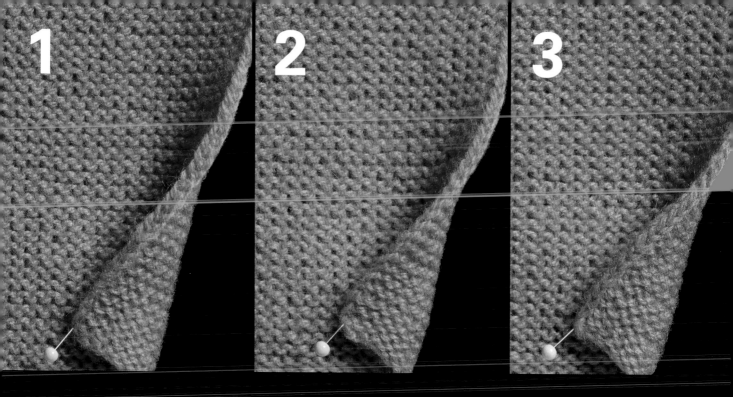

Edge stitches that won't be joined at the sides

PHOTO 1 Garter stitch. First stitch is knit through back loop, last stitch slipped purlwise with yarn in front.

PHOTO 2 Garter stitch. Slip first stitch purlwise with yarn in front, knit last stitch.

PHOTO 3 Garter stitch. Slip the last two stitches purlwise with yarn in front, knit the first two stitches. This is a good edging for scarves.

PHOTO 4 Garter stitch. On right side, slip the second stitch from edge with yarn behind and purl on wrong side. Knit the outermost stitch at each side on every row. This edge stitch method is good for scarves and button/buttonhole bands.

PHOTO 5 K2, p2 ribbing. The third stitch from the edge is a foldline stitch which stabilizes the edge.

PHOTO 6 K1, p1 ribbing. The second stitch in functions as a foldline stitch and makes a fine edge.

WORK AS FOLLOWS • On the right side: Work an edge stitch, slip 1 stitch purlwise with yarn behind, work *K1, p1*. Repeat * to * and end the row with k1, slip 1 purlwise with yarn behind, 1 edge stitch.

On the wrong side: Begin the row with 1 edge stitch, p2, *k1, p1* and end the row with p1, 1 edge stitch. At the beginning of each row, purl the edge stitch and end the row with a twisted knit stitch.

If you prefer k2, p2 ribbing, try the following:

WORK AS FOLLOWS • On the right side: 1 edge st, k1, sl 1 purlwise with yarn behind, (k2, p2) across, ending with k2, sl 1purlwise with yarn in back, k1, 1 edge st.

On the wrong side: 1 edge st, p4, (k2, p2) across, ending the row with p2, 1 edge st. Purl the edge stitch at the beginning of the row and work a k1 through back loop at end of row.

In this case, you can work several stitches between the edge stitch and the slipped stitch depending on how wide you want the edge, the type of garment, and its quality. If you are knitting a band on a heavy cardigan, you might need to have two stitches between the edge stitch and the slipped stitch. Sample to see what works for you.

The stitches outside the foldline stitch turn in towards the wrong side and make a good facing as well as stabilizing the edge. The fold doesn't need to be sewn down.

Ribbing

Ribbing produces the effect which its name implies. Traditionally, ribbing produces its best effect by being worked back and forth. The overall look can vary depending on whether you work back and forth or in the round. Sock legs, mitten cuffs, and neckbands are usually worked in the round. Though, of course, there are exceptions to every rule ...

Ribbing is easily associated with edges on garments, knitted in stockinette or for sock legs and mittens. It's also great to work an entire garment in ribbing. Why not make a pretty cardigan with simple front bands with fine, distinct edges where the buttons shine as a little bonus? Or a sweater with a neckband, where the ribbing is unbroken as it continues up into a wider neckband? Ribbing can be worked as k1, p1; k2 p2; k3, p3; and so on. But it doesn't always have to run in straight lines.

You can certainly use a great combination of ribbing methods on one and the same garment. All the edges can be worked in one technique, for example, ribbing with cables, while the body and sleeves are worked in regular k2, p2 ribbing.

On a ribbed garment, work all the edges with 1 U.S. or ½-1 mm size smaller needles than for the overall garment. In that case, it won't work do to make increases if the technique doesn't include them; the ribbing should be worked in straight lines. Instead, you can change to larger needles when you start the body, working the ribbing more firmly than for regular stockinette.

For scarves, which are most pleasing when they are reversible, ribbing is an excellent technique in combination with a distinct edge.

The stitch count for k1, p1 or k2, p2 ribbing should be evenly divisible by two or four; then an edge stitch is added at each side. It's important that the ribbing pattern match at the sides where it will be

Think about ...

* After working each purl stitch, tug the yarn a little extra. That way you'll get a more even and finer ribbing.

* When binding off in ribbing with the standard method, work stitches in pattern—knit over knit and purl over purl.

LEFT K1, p1 ribbing.   **RIGHT** K2, p2 ribbing.

sewn together. It doesn't look at all good when two knit stitches or two purl stitches adjoin each other at the side on an edge worked with k1, p1 ribbing.

To match the patterns elegantly in k2, p2 ribbing, place the two knit stitches on each side of the front edge. For heavier knitting, the stitches on the lower edge should align with the stitches in the neckband ribbing.

Ribbing makes a neater side seam if you sew a knit stitch to a purl stitch (so that a peak meets a valley). Also, do not sew between two garter stitches. So that the sides will match, the stitch count in k2, p2 ribbing should be an even number divisible by four and then you'll add the two edge stitches to use for sewing up plus an edge stitch at each side. In practice, this means that, inside the edge stitches, you should work two knit stitches at the beginning and end of one piece and, correspondingly, two purl stitches on the other piece so that the patterns will match afterwards.

CABLE RIBS

K2, p2 ribbing with cables makes a pleasing effect in an otherwise plain garment. The stitch count should be an even number divisible by 4 + 1 edge stitch at each side and stitches needed for assembly.

LEFT K2, p2 ribbing with cables crossed on every fourth row. **RIGHT** K3, p3 ribbing moving one stitch to the right on every eigth row.

WORK AS FOLLOWS • Work back and forth: Row 1 on right side: 1 edge st, *k2tog, leave sts on left needle and knit the first st once more. Drop the two sts off left needle, p2*. Repeat * to *. End with 1 edge st. Rows 2-4: Work in k2, p2 ribbing as set over sts of Row 1. Repeat Rows 1-4.

If you began with a chain-style cast-on, you can begin the cable on the first row on the right side. If you used long-tail cast-on, then the first row is always on the wrong side and the cable is begun on the next, right side, row.

Work the last row of ribbing on the right side, with Row 1. The stockinette stitch then begins on the wrong side with a purl row. This applies whether you used a chain or long-tail cast-on.

STAGGERED RIBS

Staggered ribs can be worked with 2-2, 3-3, 2-3, 3-4 stitches, etc. Work the specified number of rows and then shift the pattern one stitch sideways and then work the same number of rows to the next shift. This applies even at the transition from the edge to stockinette. You can work the ribs to slant to the right or to the left. In general, staggered ribs are a little looser than regular ribs so you need to swatch to make sure you'll get the result you want. Tube socks are an example of a garment worked completely in staggered ribbing.

K2, p2 ribbing worked with two colors in standard two-color stranded knitting.

TWO-COLOR RIBS

You can work either k1, p1 or k2, p2 ribbing with two colors. One color is used for the vertical knit stitch lines and the other color for the purl lines. Hold the strands as you usually do for two-color stranded knitting. The dominant color is placed over the index finger and under the middle finger and the other strand, nearest the fingernail, over both the index and middle fingers.

Two-color ribs will not have the same elasticity as regular ribbing but still produce a nice effect. After the cast-on row, you'll need to start with a set-up row (see page 125) with the two colors all worked as knit stitches on the right side. On the following row, you can begin the two-color ribbing. The knitted set-up row means that you'll avoid those unattractive dots of color that occur when you purl over a different color. To simplify matters, work the ribbing in the round.

TWISTED RIBS

Twisted ribs are used, for the most part, with inelastic yarns. Twisted ribbing is worked back and forth as either single 1-1 ribs or double 2-2 ribs. A stitch is twisted when it's worked through the back loop. Usually every other *vertical* stitch line is twisted which means that the rib-

LEFT 1-1 twisted ribbing, non-reversible. RIGHT 2-2 twisted ribbing, non-reversible.

bing will be different on each side. On the wrong side, the purl stitches are twisted and, on the right side, the knit stitches are twisted. On the wrong side, the ribbing will look like as usual while the right side has obvious vertical stripes where the knit stitches stand out.

Normally, you can expect twisted ribbing to be a little firmer than regular ribbing. Sample to get the results you want.

For all twisted, non-reversible ribbing, the ribs will look like regular ribs on one side. You can choose which side to consider as the right side but decide this right at the beginning because the cast-on row will also have a right side (see pages 32-44).

WORK AS FOLLOWS • Example of 1-1, non-reversible, twisted ribbing. Row 1, on wrong side: 1 edge st, *p1tbl, k1*. Repeat * to * and end with 1 edge st. Row 2, on right side: 1 edge st, *p1, k1tbl*. Rep * to * and end with 1 edge st.

On each side, it's the same stitch which is twisted in a vertical line. Personally, I think that the side with the twisted stitches is the most pleasing and can give a simple garment that little something extra! Errors most often occur when the knit stitches are twisted on every row. This means that the piece should be worked in the round to be correct. If, instead, you work back and forth and twist all the knit stitches, the ribs will be uneven and produce an unattractive effect with alternating twisted and untwisted stitches up the vertical lines.

Twisted ribs can also be worked to be *reversible*, which means that the same stitch is always twisted. The technique is most often used for stiff and inelastic yarns, such as linen. The effect will be pleasing but this type of ribbing is hard to knit.

• Increasing within ribbing—79.

Think about ...

✳ When binding off a twisted rib, twist the stitches in pattern even on this row.

✳ If you have trouble working the purl stitches through the back loop, you can turn the stitch clockwise and place it back on the left needle. Now purl the stitch as usual.

Twisted reversible 1-1 ribbing worked with linen yarn.

Edges for Various Parts of a Garment

The most common edges for the lower part of a body, on the sleeves, and around the neck are various types of ribbing (see pages 60-65). However, there are a number of other fine solutions in the form of doubled edges, garter stitch edges, rolled edges of various types, and more. It's important to choose an edge, whether single or double, that will suit your garment. What is it that you want to knit? What yarn will be used and which techniques?

The width of an edge can vary. In general, the lower edge of a garment body and the sleeve edges are the same width, while the neckband is narrower. It doesn't have to always be that way, though. Sometimes it's better if the sleeve cuffs are wider than the body's lower edge. As always, sample to see what works for you.

It's also important that you knit a swatch of the actual edge. Which needles are most suitable? Will the edge be folded and sewn down afterwards or will it be attached as it's knitted? How do you accommodate the edge stitches at the side seam when it will be sewn together? What about the increases between the edge and the rest of the knitting? There are many details to think about before you start knitting.

If you are uncertain, it's a sure bet to use the same edge at the lower edge of the body as for the sleeves and to finish the neck edge. This creates a nice symmetry and the garment will have a pleasing overall effect.

Here are a few suggestions for how you can make simple, pretty edges, how you can work neat increases, and how to control the edge stitches at the sides so the seaming will be fine. In the introduction to the book, you can read about the importance of encircling the garment as a whole and learn about what a key factor and how important edges are for a pleasing finished result. It isn't hard!

DOUBLED EDGE IN STOCKINETTE WITH A KNIT FOLDLINE

Cast on provisionally so that you can release the stitches later on, using either a crochet cord of chain stitches to pick up stitches from or work a few rows with cotton yarn to use as a base for the cast-on row (see page 39 and following).

Begin by working the section of the edge that will later be folded in and sewn to the wrong side of the garment. Use smaller needles than

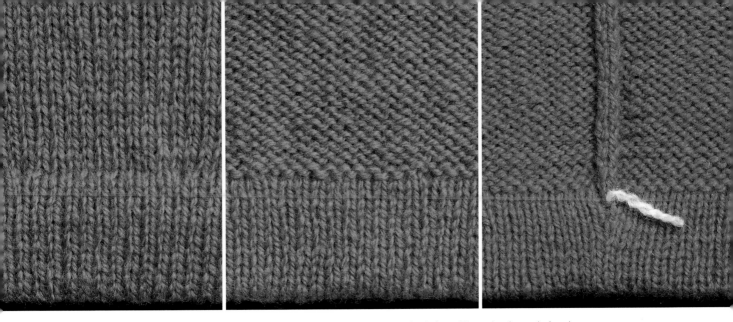

A doubled edge with a stockinette foldline and increased stitches. The edge has a knitted join and the side seam sewn afterwards. **LEFT** Right side. **CENTER** Wrong side. **RIGHT** Side seam on wrong side.

for the stockinette edge on the right side—1 U.S. size or ½-1 mm size smaller.

SAMPLE • Cast on stitches. Work 14 rows in stockinette, beginning with a knit row (a total of 15 rows including the cast-on row). Knit one row with a larger needle—at least 2 U.S. sizes / 1½ mm larger. This row will be looser and form a foldline; it's knit on the right side. Work 15 rows in stockinette as for the inside of the doubled edge, with the smaller needles. Work the last row on the *wrong* side.

If you want a wider or narrower edge, you can easily calculate what row to begin knitting on. Get out your paper and pencil and mark the wrong-side rows with a horizontal line and the right-side rows with a vertical line. Begin by drawing a horizontal line corresponding to the last row on the wrong side. Alternate vertical and horizontal lines for as many rows as you want the edge to be wide. Mark a foldline that will be worked on larger needles and then continue to mark out the rows on the folded section. The last line corresponds to the stitches to be picked up.

If you want an even number of rows in the edge, begin with a knit row. In that case, the foldline on the larger needles will be on the wrong side and purled because the last, even-numbered row must be worked on the wrong side. The reason for this is that it's easier to join the edge on the right side.

Purl foldline

Cast-on

Stockinette, loosely knitted foldline

Cast-on

When it's time to join the edge, take a smaller needle and pick up the stitches (the bars between stitch loops of the cast-on edge) at the same time removing the crochet chain (or the extras rows with cotton yarn). If you prefer, you can use double-pointed needles and work in stages with a smaller number of stitches at a time. There will be one stitch less on this needle because you are picking up between the stitches from the provisional cast-on and not the stitches themselves. Double check!

Fold the edge with wrong side facing wrong side. Hold the needle with the picked-up stitches behind the needle with live stitches. Work with right side facing, and begin with a knit (edge) stitch from the front section/needle and then knit together a stitch from the front needle with a stitch from the back needle. At the end of the row, separately work a stitch from the back needle and then one from the front needle. All of the stitches, including the edge stitches are knitted. Both outermost stitches from the front section/needle now function as edge stitches and are ready to use when it comes time to seam the sides.

DOUBLED EDGE IN STOCKINETTE WITH A PURL FOLDLINE

The foldline in a doubled edge can also be worked with purl stitches on the right side or knit stitches on the wrong side. This method more clearly delineates the fold on the right side. This row is also counted in the number of rows on the right side of the edge. There should be the same number of rows on both sides on the fold and the foldline is always included with the count for the front. Use the same size needles for the entire edge. Begin knitting with the part of the edge that will later be folded in and sewn to the wrong side of the garment.

The cast-on, decreases, and possible increases are worked the same way as for a doubled edge with a stockinette foldline (see page 66).

SAMPLE • Cast on stitches. Work in stockinette for 15 rows; the cast-on row counts as a knit row and is included in the 15-row count. Work one knit row on the wrong side with the same size needle as for the edge as a whole. This will be the foldline. Continue in stockinette for 14 rows (= 15 rows with the foldline included). The last row is worked on the wrong side.

Remove the crocheted chain and place the "stitches" (which actually

Doubled edge with purled foldline and increases stitches. Edge knitted to join.

are the bars between stitches on the cast-on edge) onto a smaller needle. If you prefer, you can use double-pointed needles and work in stages with a smaller number of stitches at a time.

Think about ...

✳ If you making a doubled edge, it's important that neither section be wider than the other and "create excess."

✳ The stockinette foldline is worked with a larger needle and lies horizontally centered at the fold while a purl foldline, together with the row preceding it, forms a fold that looks like a V. So that the fold will lie flat and smooth, the number of rows must be adjusted depending on what type of foldline you'll use (see above).

✳ Don't forget to count the cast-on row in the row counts!

✳ When sewing the side seams on an edge joined by knitting, begin on the right side on the lower edge at the fold. Let a bit of the yarn hang freely and sew inside one edge stitch on each side, from the bottom up. Take the other end of the yarn and sew the fold of the edge. Sew as far as it goes inside an edge stitch and then return to using ½ edge stitch as the seam allowance. Try to make the seam as flat and smooth as possible.

EDGE FOLDED AND SEWN DOWN AFTERWARDS

In the previous examples, the edge was folded double and knitted together as the work proceeded. If, instead, you want to fold up the edge

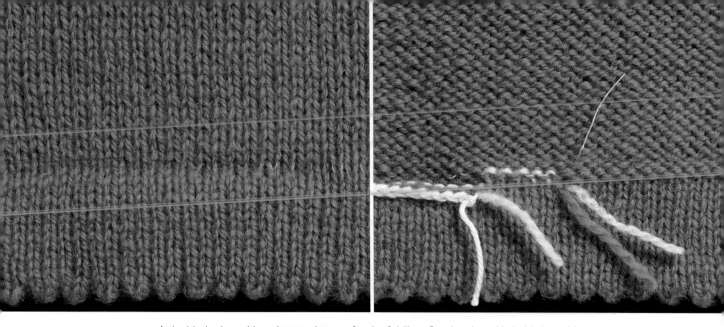

A doubled edge with a picot eyelet row for the foldline. Sewing thread is held alongside the yarn on the joining row to make it easier to see where to sew the stitches. **LEFT** Right side. **RIGHT** Wrong side.

and sew it down after you've seamed the sides, work as follows: Cast on and work as described in the samples above, but, work the section of the edge that will be sewn to the wrong side with one less row. On the first stockinette row on the right side, corresponding to the row to be joined, carry a length of contrast-color sewing thread with the yarn. This will help you see where to sew when you sew the edge down with duplicate stitch during finishing. The sewing thread is then removed. The row you finish with on the inside of the edge will be the row that you'll sew the edge to. You should also sew so that each stitch lies on the lower edge of the joining row. Visualize how the edge should look as you sew the facing down.

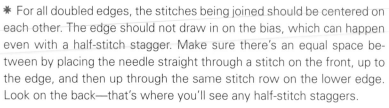

Think about ...

✴ It's easier to sew the side seams if you fold and sew down the edge afterwards, although it will be a little trickier to do the sewing up.

✴ It's easier to join the edge while knitting. This also produces the best result.

✴ For all doubled edges, the stitches being joined should be centered on each other. The edge should not draw in on the bias, which can happen even with a half-stitch stagger. Make sure there's an equal space between by placing the needle straight through a stitch on the front, up to the edge, and then up through the same stitch row on the lower edge. Look on the back—that's where you'll see any half-stitch staggers.

A rolled edge worked over four rows.

On the first right side row—here called the "joining row"—you can also work any needed increases. Take the increases into consideration when sewing down the edge.

ROLLED EDGE

A rolled edge is an edge that forms a little roll at the lower edge of a garment. It's nice to use in combination with stockinette where the yarn and edge give a completed look to the garment and it works well for sweaters knit with finer yarn. This edge has a tendency to draw in, so you should sample it by using the same size needles and stitch count as for the stockinette.

SAMPLE • With the long-tail method, cast on an even number of stitches. Rows 1, 3, 5, on the wrong side: 1 edge st, *slip 1 purlwise with yarn behind (i.e., on right side of fabric), p1*. Repeat * to *, ending with 1 edge st. Rows 2, 4, 6, right side: 1 edge st, *k1, slip 1 purlwise with yarn in front of the stitch (on right side of fabric)*. Repeat * to *, ending with 1 edge st.

The stitches that, on the right side, look like stockinette are worked on every row; the "purl" stitches are slipped purlwise on every row with the yarn on the right side. Look on the wrong side and you'll clearly see that the slipped stitches are not caught and won't be until you start the stockinette part of the work. The edge is worked with four rows and it

Rolled edge, four rolls with slipped stitches work over six rows and with two rows of stockinette between each roll. **LEFT** Right side. **RIGHT** Wrong side.

makes a smaller, less firm roll. The number of rows can be adjusted for the yarn and needle size you are using. The thicker the yarn, the fewer the rows.

If you want an edge with several rolls, one after the other, you can try another, somewhat softer cast-on. Pick up half the stitch count from a crocheted chain and then, after a few rows in stockinette, remove the chain and, with an extra needle, pick up the loops in between (now stitches) from the cast-on row. Fold the edge to the wrong side and knit a stitch from each needle, thus doubling the number of stitches. The needle with one more stitch faces the right side. This lower edge makes the first "row" when you want to knit several rolls, one after the other. Work two rows of stockinette between each "roll." Use needles 1 U.S. / ½ mm size smaller for these two rows. On the rolls, the same stitch is always slipped.

If you are working in the round, cast on an extra stitch when the cast-on edge is finished so that you have an even number of stitches for the rolls.

Cable cast-on. Garter stitch edge with increases in the stitches of previous row, on the wrong side.

Think about ...

✳ To have neater sides for seaming, slip the first and last stitch inside the edge stitch on on each side. This applies to both the back and front pieces. If you want to use this method, make sure you have an odd number of stitches.

✳ To avoid sewing the edges at the side seam, you can cast on an even number of stitches and work the entire lower edge on a circular needle. Next, divide the work into the pieces, add an edge stitch on each side, and then work each piece separately, back and forth.

GARTER STITCH EDGE

A garter stitch edge is a sure thing on a simple, perhaps rather straight, sweater. You don't need a very wide edge to hold it in and to keep the garment within the circle. A garter stitch edge should have fewer stitches because the technique spreads out widthwise. Even if you want the edge to be rather straight, you should use smaller needles and fewer stitches. Swatch the edge with some stockinette and block the swatch so you can see how many stitches you have in 4 in / 10 cm and work your calculations from there.

Garter stitch should always be knitted a little more firmly than, for example, stockinette. It combines well with texture patterns, the cable cast-on method, and the one over two bind-off.

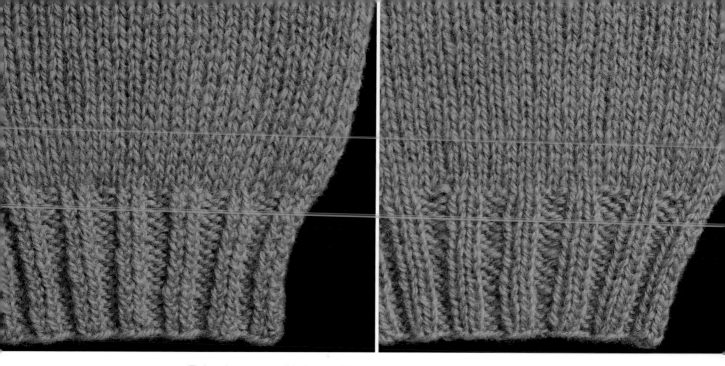

LEFT Twisted, non-reversible k2, p2 ribbing. Increases are made in the strands between two knit stitches. All the increases face the same direction as the slant of the twisted stitches. **RIGHT** K2, p2 ribbing. Increases are made in the strands between two purl stitches. The strand is twisted to slant towards the closest side of the piece.

RIBBED EDGE

For a ribbed edge, we recommend a smaller number of stitches than for the rest of the knitting. The number of stitches depends a little on the quality and type of the yarn you are using, so sample. If your pattern has the same number of stitches for the both the ribbed edge and the stockinette, don't be afraid to change it. The ribbing can also be worked on smaller needles, about 1-2 U.S. or ½-1 mm sizes smaller than for the rest of the knitting in the garment.

Ribbing can be worked with k1, p1; k2, p2; k3, p3; and so on, but doesn't need to be worked in straight lines or have the same number of knit stitches as purl stitches in the ribbing. For edges in staggered ribbing, ribs with cables, or twisted rib, the same rules apply as for standard ribbing—work with fewer stitches and smaller needles than for the rest of the piece.

Traditionally, k1, p1 ribbing is recommended for thinner and finer garments and double ribbing (k2, p2) for heavier and thicker sportswear. I think this is a question of taste. Usually k2, p2 ribbing is more even and finer and produces a better effect even for fine knitting. Tug a little more after each purl stitch and work the ribbing back and forth.

Increases

There's no general rule for increasing. The most important thing is that the increases are neat and fine, lean in the correct direction, and don't produce unwanted holes in the piece. An increase should blend into the rest of the knitting smoothly.

There are several different ways to increase and it's important that you try them all to find out which is best for the case at hand. The choice varies depending on technique, gauge, and quality of the yarn. Sometimes the effects of the increases aren't visible until the sample has been blocked, so sample several increases on your gauge swatch.

The most common method for increasing is to increase into the previous row (RLI or LLI) or to lift the strand between two stitches and then knit it through the back loop (M1). These increases can be used in different ways depending on the look of the knitting.

Sometimes, the instructions might suggest that you increase in the same stitch by first knitting into the front loop of the stitch and then knitting into the back loop of the same stitch (k1f&b). This makes a "purl" stitch or a little knot on the right side of the work, which might be acceptable if it's made as a conscious and *evenly repeated* effect, as, for example, on a thumb gusset. In other circumstances, it can totally ruin an otherwise lovely piece of knitting.

You can increase on either the right or wrong side but need to make sure that the stitch leans in the correct direction and that the stitch is worked correctly as garter, knit or purl. Look on the right side before you continue knitting to make sure that the increases look good.

In garter stitch, you can increase both in the strands between stitches and in the stitches of the previous row. Often it's an advantage to increase on the *wrong* side. Test the options to see what works best for your knitting. In stockinette, it's easiest to increase on the right side for the increases in the stitch of the row below and to make 1 in the strand between two stitches, but either works just as well on the right and wrong sides. Generally, there's no real difference, but you should always check to make sure the increases lean in the correct direction.

If you have an odd-number of rows between the increases, the increases will be worked, alternately, on the right side and on the wrong side. If you want to avoid this, adjust the number of rows between increases: one time, work one row less, and the next time, work one row more. If, for example, you want to increase on every seventh row, you can, instead, alternate increasing on every sixth and then eighth row, both on the right side.

Increases in a pattern should be made so that they blend in as well as possible. Increases should be placed so that they will look best with the pattern but be as invisible as possible.

When it comes to increasing at the sides as well as increasing between an edge and stockinette, it's a good idea to divide the increases out from the center of the piece and increase half the number of stitches leaning towards one direction/side and the other half of the increases leaning in the opposite direction. There will be a clear difference and effect which can also differ in various styles of knitting depending on the quality, technique, and gauge.

NOTE: When I mention right and left below, you should visualize looking at the work right in front of you as you would see it when knitting—on the right or wrong side of the piece.

INCREASING IN STRAND BETWEEN STITCHES—MAKE 1

ON THE RIGHT SIDE • You can increase by lifting the strand between two stitches with the left needle tip and then knitting into the back loop.

Increasing in the strand between two stitches with right side facing. The right leg of the strand lies at the front and slants to the left. Insert the needle into the back of the loop and knit the stitch = M1L (make 1 left).

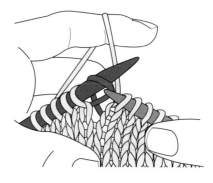

Increasing in the strand between two stitches with right side facing. The left leg of the strand lies at the front and slants to the right. Insert the needle into the front of the loop and knit the stitch = M1R (make 1 right).

This increase can be made with either the right or left leg of the strand lying in front of the needle. Sample both of these special cases to see which slant will look best on each side of the knitting. It's most common to have the left leg of the strand in front of the needle and for the increase to lean to the right on the right side of the piece, and for the right leg of the strand to lie in front and lean to the left on the left side of the piece.

ON THE WRONG SIDE • On the wrong side, the strand is twisted opposite the direction on the right side and the stitches are purled if you are working in stockinette. At the beginning of the row, the right leg of the strand is in front and, at the end of the row, the left leg is in front. Look on the right side to make sure the slant leans in the correct direction.

On a ribbed edge, when increasing stitches between the edge and stockinette, work out from the center of the row. Work the increases slanting towards each respective side and increase between two purl stitches or right after a purl stitch. This applies to all ribbing except for twisted rib (see page 79).

Think about …

… if you increase without twisting the strand between two stitches, you'll make an unwanted hole.

INCREASING IN STITCH OF PREVIOUS ROW — RIGHT- AND LEFT-LIFTED INCREASES

(See illustrations on next page.)

ON THE RIGHT SIDE • You can increase by making a stitch into a stitch on the previous row.

At the right side (at the beginning of the row where the increase should lean to the right), work *up to* the stitch where you'll make the increase. Insert the right needle into the stitch which is directly below the first stitch on the left needle and knit into that stitch = right-lifted/right-leaning increase or RLI. Continue working across/around.

At the left side (at the end of the row where the increase should lean to the left), knit to and including the stitch where you'll make the increase. Now insert the needle into the stitch below the one which you just dropped off the needle (that is, into the second stitch loop below

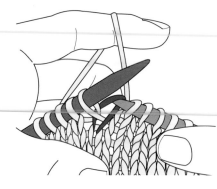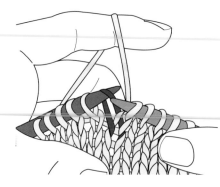

Increasing with right side facing and into the stitch of previous row. Knit the stitch. The increase slants to the right = RLI (right-lifted/right-leaning increase).

Increasing with right side facing and into the stitch below. The increase slants to the left = LLI (left-lifted/left-leaning increase).

the needle) and knit into that stitch = left-lifted/left-leaning increase or LLI.

ON THE WRONG SIDE • Increases on the wrong side are worked the same way except that the stitches are purled if you are working in stockinette.

Think about ...

✽ Sometimes, in stockinette, it's easier to catch the stitch on the wrong side.

✽ When increasing between the edge and stockinette, work out from the center and slant increases towards each respective side.

INCREASING WITH YARNOVER
A yarnover increase is used in knitting where holes are desirable; this is the foundation of lace knitting. You can make a yarnover on the right needle very easily and then, when you work the stitch on the next row, a hole is formed. Make several yarnovers in a row if you want an especially large stitch or hole.

INCREASING BETWEEN RIBBING AND STOCKINETTE
In the transition from a ribbed edge to stockinette, you can increase with M1 (make 1) on the first stockinette row on the right side. In 1-1

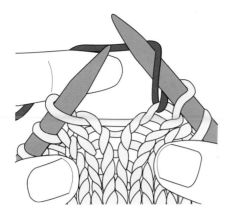

Increasing with a yarnover.

ribbing, increase on the right side *after* the purl stitch with the left side of the lifted strand at the front of the needle. On the left side, increase *before* the purl stitch with the right leg of the loop at the front. In 2-2 ribbing, increase *between* two purl stitches and twist the strand so that it slants to the respective side. In other words, at the right slide, the left leg of the strand is on the front and, at the left side, the right leg of the strand is at the front. Determine the direction of the increases out from the center of the row.

INCREASING BETWEEN NON-REVERSIBLE, TWISTED RIBBING AND STOCKINETTE

In the transition from a non-reversible, twisted rib to stockinette, on the first row of stockinette, work the knit stitches that were twisted in the ribbing also as twisted knit stitches. The increases will then follow the direction of the twisted stitches. Otherwise, the same principles apply as for all other types of ribbing except for 2-2 ribbing. In that case, the increases are worked *between* the two knit stitches. With right side facing, increase with M1 so that the right leg of the strand lies on the front of the needle. All of the increases will slant in the same direction as for the twisted stitches when the twisted side is the right side of the fabric.

In practice, this means that the purl stitches in the ribbing are knitted and the twisted knit stitches are worked as twisted knits. Use the *same size* needles as for the ribbing. With this method, you'll get an amazingly fine result in the transition between ribbing and stockinette with the twisted stitches lying on "level"—in the same line as—the purl stitches in the ribbing to make a sharp, clear line which gives the garment character without making a fuss about it.

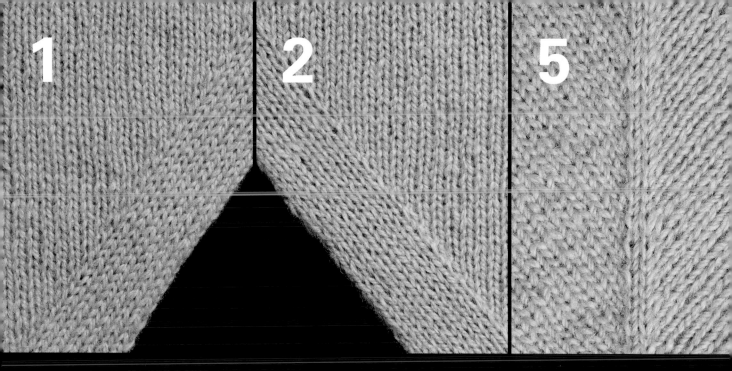

Increasing in the strand between stitches

All the increases are worked on every other row, that is, on right side rows when you are working back and forth. When you increase in the strand between stitches (M1), with stitches leaning to the right and left, you are combining 1 and 2 or 3 and 4 as shown in the examples above. The last-mentioned combination is used in all of the examples in the book.

PHOTO 1 Make 1 increase. Slants to the right. The right leg of the strand lies on front of needle.

PHOTO 2 Make 1 increase. Slants to the left. The left leg of the strand lies on front of needle.

PHOTO 3 Make 1 increase. Slants to the right. The left leg of the strand lies on front of needle.

PHOTO 4 Make 1 increase. Slants to the left. The right leg of the strand lies on front of needle.

PHOTO 5 Increasing on each side of the two center stitches. Before the first center stitch, the left leg of the strand is at the front; after the center stitch, the right leg of the strand is at the front.

PHOTO 6 Increasing on each side of the two center stitches. Before the first center stitch, the right leg of the strand is at the front; after the center stitch, the left leg of the strand is at the front.

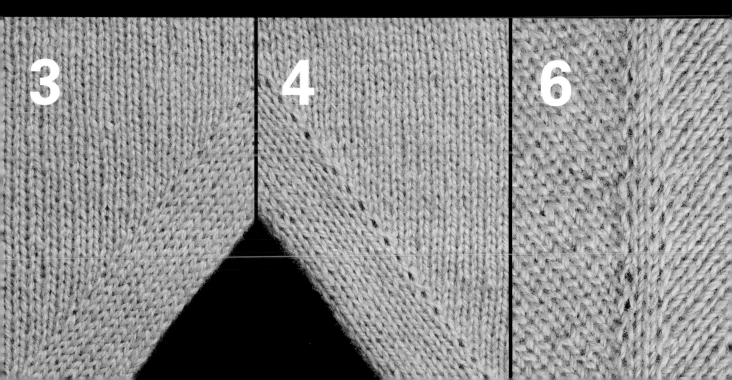

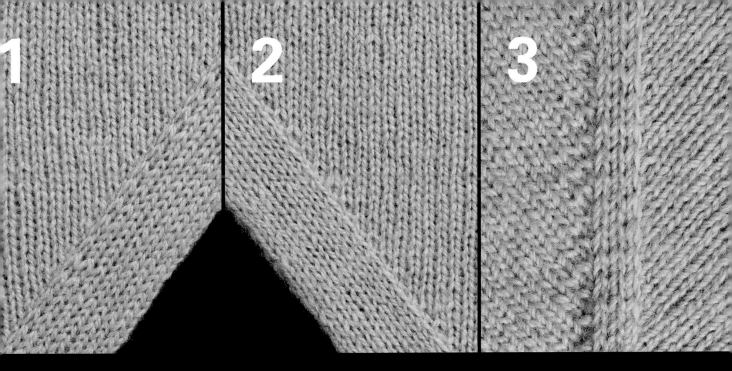

Increasing in stitch of previous row

The increases are all made on every other row, that is, on the right side rows when you are working back and forth.

PHOTO 1 Increasing in stitch of previous row. Slants to the right.

PHOTO 2 Increasing in stitch of previous row. Slants to the left.

PHOTO 3 Increasing in stitches of previous row on each side of the two center stitches. Before the center stitches, the increases slant to the left; after the center stitches, the increases slant to the right. This makes a row of three stitches in the center that slant in the opposite direction of the knitting.

PHOTO 4 Increasing in stitches of previous row on each side of the two center stitches. Before the center stitches, the increases slant to the right; after the center stitches, the increases slant to the left. Note that this makes a stitch in the center point in the opposite direction of the rest of the knitting.

Increasing with a yarnover

PHOTO 5 Increasing with a yarnover on each side of 2, 3, 1, and then 5 center stitches.

Increasing in the same stitch

PHOTO 6 Increasing by knitting into the front and then back of the same stitch. This increase should be used for an evenly recurring sequence.

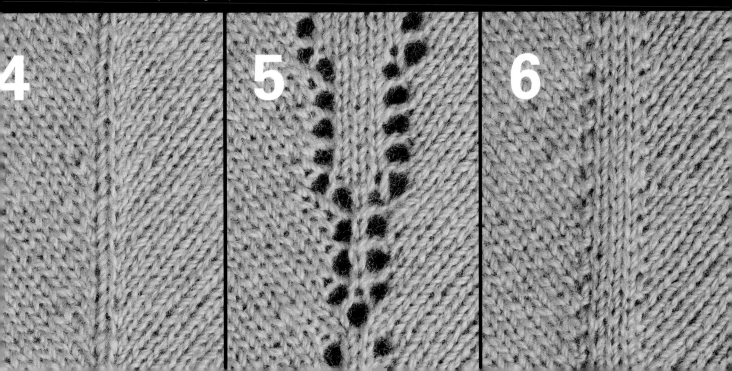

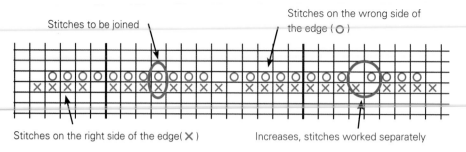

Stitches to be joined

Stitches on the wrong side of the edge (O)

Stitches on the right side of the edge(X)

Increases, stitches worked separately

Knitting to join a folded edge with increases

INCREASING BETWEEN A FOLDED EDGE AND STOCKINETTE

If you've made a folded edge in stockinette and want to increase the stitch count in the transition from the edge to the rest of the sweater, you can do this at the same time as knitting together the sets of stitches. With right side facing, begin with the edge stitch and then knit together one stitch from the front needle with one stitch with the back needle. When you want to increase, work the back and front stitches separately; in stockinette, knit both stitches. Make sure that the increases are made so that there will be an even number of stitches at each side, as calculated from the center. End with an edge stitch from the front needle. The increases will look nice and blend into the knitting.

INCREASING BEWEEN A GARTER STITCH EDGE AND STOCKINETTE

If you've worked a garter stitch edge, increase the stitch count on the last knitted row—on the wrong side. Increase into the stitches of the previous row, slanting the increases to the respective side out from the center. The increase stitches should all be knitted. Now change to larger needles and continue in stockinette, beginning on the right side.

Maybe you're one of the knitters who gets a better result if you increase on the wrong side with M1 (lifting strand between stitches and then knitting into strand)—sample. Don't forget to slant the increases towards the respective sides.

INCREASING BETWEEN A ROLLED EDGE AND STOCKINETTE

If you've made a rolled edge, you generally will not need to increase the stitch count between the rolled edge, with every other stitch worked, and stockinette. All you have to do is simply change to stockinette. If you want to increase, do so as invisibly as possible.

Decreases

When you are going to make decreases in your work and the instructions mention the right or left side, you should look at the work from straight in front, on the right or wrong side. You shouldn't worry about which will be the right or left side when you'll be wearing the garment.

No matter where they occur in the garment, the decreases should blend in and be as invisible and neat as possible. It's always easiest to decrease on the right side but all decreases can be made on the wrong side—just make sure that they slant in the correct direction and that the stitch is worked correctly as garter, stockinette, or purl and isn't twisted. Check the right side to make sure that the result looks good. Decreases within a pattern should be suited to the technique and pattern in the best way possible.

DECREASING ON THE RIGHT SIDE

AT THE BEGINNING OF A ROW • Turn the two outermost stitches on the left needle so they are open. Knit them together through the back loops (before turning the front) stitch loop. This decrease is abbreviated as ssk—slip, slip, knit.

On the right side: slip the first stitch from the left to right needle as if to knit; slip the second stitch the same way. Slide the stitches back to the left needle. Now the front legs of the loops lie at the back of the left needle. Knit both stitches together through the back loops. This decrease, ssk, slants left and corresponds to knit 1-slip 1-pass slipped stitch over.

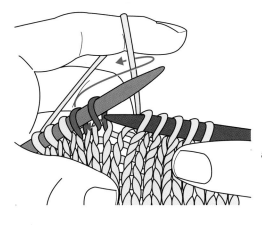

Slip, slip, knit. The stitches are knitted together through back loops. This decrease leans to the left.

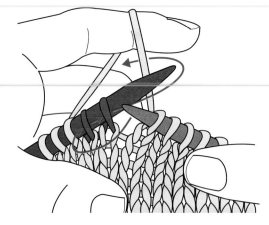

Two stitches knitted together. This decrease slants right.

NOTE: Sometimes the instructions say that you should slip a stitch, knit a stitch, and pass the slipped stitch over the knitted one. A long, unattractive stitch will be visible in the knitting which can't be pulled into position and won't disappear after blocking. The instructions might also suggest that you should knit two stitches together through the back loops. This makes an even more unattractive effect in your knitting because the visible stitch on the right side will be twisted. For a raglan shaping with decreases on every other row, one stitch will be twisted and the other open in the stitch line that runs from the armhole to the neck.

AT THE END OF THE ROW • Knit two stitches together. This decrease slants right.

Depending on how you want the decreases to slant on your garment, you can let the decreases change sides so that you work two stitches together at the beginning of the row and ssk at the end.

DECREASING ON THE WRONG SIDE

At the beginning of the row, purl two stitches together. At the end, the two outermost stitches on the left needle are turned and slipped. Slip the first stitch on the left needle to the right needle as if to knit and then slip the next stitch the same way. Insert the left needle through both stitches, slide the stitches to the left needle and purl them together. The stitches have now changed places and are open. Check the right side to make sure the decrease is correct. For garter stitch, you can use the same method, but knit the stitches together.

Decreasing two stitches at the same time. The center stitch lies on top.

DOUBLE DECREASE

When you need to decrease two stitches at the same time, as, for example, in a ribbed edge on a V-neck, on raglan sleeves, or some details in lace knitting, it can be good to knit three stitches together so that the center stitch lies on top, facing the right side to form a straight and distinct line.

Sometimes the instructions will say to decrease one stitch on each side of a center stitch. That leaves a center "single" stitch with long strands on each side from the decreases. Do this instead.

ON THE RIGHT SIDE • Slip two stitches to the right needle as if to be knitted together, slip another single stitch knitwise to the right needle. Insert the left needle from the back and towards the front, through all three stitches and use the right needle to catch the yarn from the wrong side to make a new stitch. The center stitch should lie on top on the right side. Tighten the yarn. If this is a little difficult, you can slip two stitches to the right needles as if to knit together, knit the next stitch and pass the two slipped stitches over the knitted one.

ON THE WRONG SIDE • Slip one stitch knitwise to the right needle, slip another stitch the same way. Slide the stitches back to the left needle so that the first stitch becomes number two on the left needle. Make sure that the center stitch lies on top on the left needle and that the stitches are not twisted. Purl the three stitches together.

These decreases can be made on both the right and wrong sides and you can slip the stitches so that the center stitch *always* lies on top, as seen

Decreases made by knitting three stitches together. The center stitch always lies on top. Stitches are decreased on every other row, or on every right side (RS) row when you are working back and forth.

from the right side, without being twisted. For ribbing on a V-neck, decrease on the right and wrong sides, even on the bind-off row. On a square neck with a 90-degree corner, decrease the same way, but on every other row.

BAND DECREASE

Band decreases are used, for example, at the top of hats, for raglan shaping, and mitten tops and sock toes. Knit two stitches together and then ssk. The decrease stitch lines now form a pleasing band next to each other.

If you are using a band decrease, you might want to embellish the band with a cable between the decreases (see photo 5 on the page opposite).

WORK AS FOLLOWS • K2tog (decrease), p1, k2 (which you can use for a cable), p1, and then ssk (decrease). Work the decreases on every other row = every right side row if you are working back and forth. For the cable: K2tog. Do not drop the stitches from the left needle; knit the first stitch again and then drop the two stitches. Cross the cable on every fourth row = every other right side row.

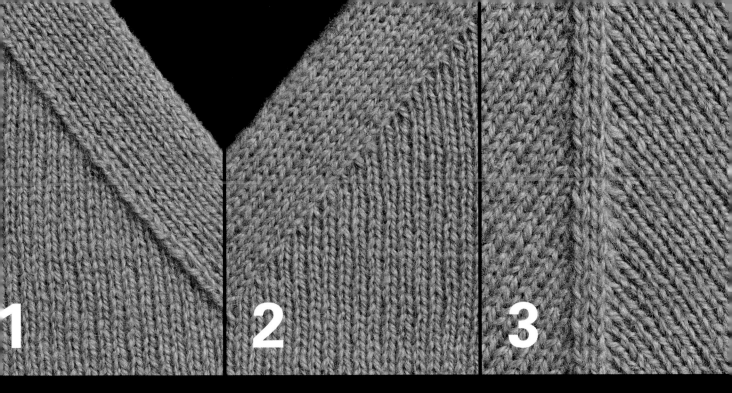

Decreases

All these decreases are worked on every other row = every right side row if you are working back and forth.

PHOTO 1 Decrease that slants to the left made with ssk.

PHOTO 2 Decrease that slants to the right made with k2tog.

PHOTO 3 Decreases at the center of a knitted piece, the so-called band decrease. In this picture, the decreases are placed next to each other.

PHOTO 4 Decreases as for Photo 3. In this case, the decreases have been used for a raglan sleeve where the body is joined with the sleeves.

PHOTO 5 Band decrease with a cable between the decreases.

Swirl decrease—decreases all worked as knit two together. The decreases are worked on every other row = every right side row when working back and forth.

SWIRL DECREASE

For a swirl decrease, divide the total stitch count into equal sections so that the decreases can be made at the dividing line between each section. For each decrease row, decrease the number of stitches in each section by one stitch. The same stitch is always at the front of the decreases and forms a nice line in the knitting.

Swirl deceasing can be made to slant either to the right or the left. Which direction will depend on how you choose to work the decreases. Swirl decreasing is very effective on hats, and tams, with their flat tops provide a nice surface for the swirls. This method of decreasing is also a good choice for knitting round pillows and can even be used for shaping a mitten or sock.

Side Seams

For most side seams, it's important that you have an edge stitch on every row (see Edge stitches, page 55). The exceptions are those techniques with rows that don't lengthen in proportion to the stitches and so would become wavy if an edge stitch is worked on every row.

Use the length of yarn hanging at the cast-on edge to sew with; the length should be three times the length of the seam. Use a blunt, bent tip, tapestry. If the yarn is too short, but is wool, you can splice the yarn by moistening it and rubbing the ends together. With any other fiber, you should fasten off the ends with a needle and start with a new strand.

Side seams are sewn together with the *right side facing*, from the bottom up. Lay the pieces edge to edge on your knee. Place your left hand, with the palm up, *centered* on the seam with the cast-on edge away from you. With your index finger under the left side and the middle finger under the right side, you can then simply use your thumb and the tapestry needle to open the edge stitches so you can then see where the bars between stitches are hiding.

It's easy to want to grip the whole piece with your left hand, but your hand isn't enough so train yourself to keep your hand centered on the seam. You'll see how easy it is after a little practice!

Begin sewing at the cast-on edge. Use the yarn hanging at the left side. Insert the needle from below and then up, inside the cast-on

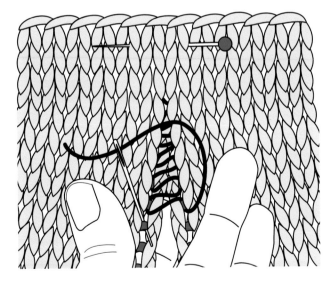

The side seam in stockinette. The drawing shows how you should hold the pieces with your left hand as you sew the seam.

The work is pinned to a backing so it will stay well tensioned.

The drawing shows the seam pulled apart so you can see the stitching more clearly.

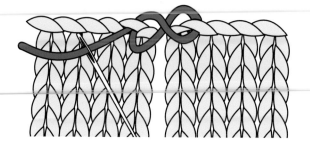

"Figure eight", the stitch for beginning and ending a side seam.

row on the right side; pull yarn through. The same way, sew a stitch up to the yarn on the left side and draw the yarn through the stitch. You should now see that a figure eight has formed around the cast-on edge inside the edge stitches. Tighten the yarn so it looks good.

Now sew through *every* bar inside each edge stitch, on the right side and then on the left side. Always sew through one bar at a time. Insert the needle down at the same place where it came up on the previous stitch, alternately on the front and on the back.

Tighten the yarn enough so that the stitch lines/rows come together well and make sure that the seam has the same elasticity as the rest of the knitting after blocking. The seam should not pucker or be so loose that it's bubbly. It's important that the yarn is adjusted all through the sewing.

Be careful to ensure that there's a straight, horizontal line in the transition between the edge and the stockinette. If this needs to be adjusted, you can do so by sewing around two strands on one side. The adjustment should be made an inch or so / a few centimeters down from the transition; otherwise, it will be visible.

Finishing is easy when you have the same number of rows or stripes in a garment. You just need to match the two sides. Along the same lines, you should ensure that increases and decreases at the sides align. Here's where marking threads are handy. To more easily see the details in your knitting, you can hold the piece up to the light. Sometimes it doesn't align properly so you can make one stitch around two bars at the side to adjust.

Up at the underarm, you might need to fiddle a bit with the stitches, sewing just enough to make it smooth and neat. When you've sewn the seam up to the underarm, end by making a figure eight as for the beginning of the seam.

Think about ...

❋ You'll achieve a straighter and neater line if you sew around a bar between stitches one at a time.

❋ One tried and true old trick to use when sewing facings on fabric or seams (and, in this case, a side seam in knitting), is to sit comfortably with your legs crossed, and attach the knitting—the lower part of the seam—to your pants with a pin. Then it will be very easy to tension the piece for an even seam. As you work, move the piece and pin so that the position of the work is comfortable.

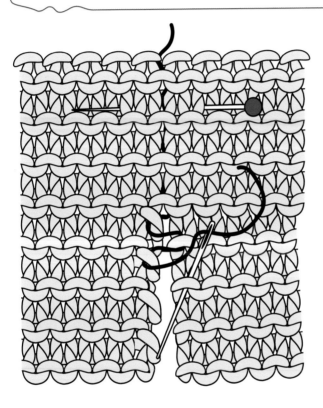

A side seam on garter stitch. The work is pinned to a backing for better tensioning. The stitches are sewn with a blunt tip needle, preferably one with a bent tip.

Two garter stitch pieces are sewn together in the same way except that, on one side, you sew into the *center* of the outermost stitch and, on the other side, sew *between* two stitches—both inside the edge stitch. This means that, on one side, you are sewing into the loop that points *downwards* in the knitting (bar) and, on the other side, you sew into the loop pointing *upwards* in the knitting (stitch). Practically speaking, it means that you sew into the part where the stitch and bar lie on a little ridge on the right side. Do not sew into the "valley."

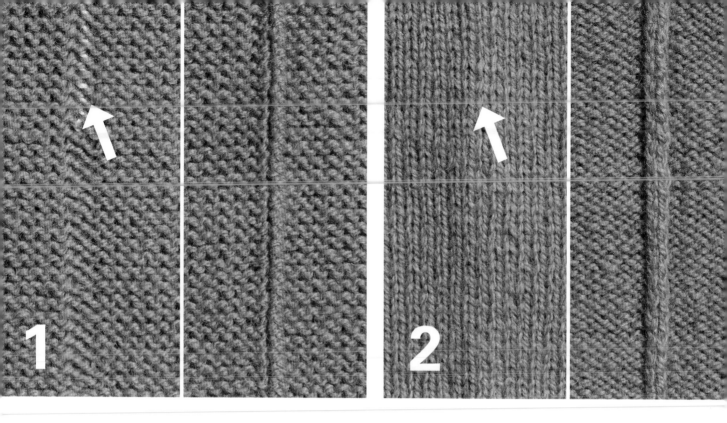

PHOTO 1 Side seam in garter stitch. An edge stitch is knitted on every row, at both beginning and end of the row. **LEFT** Right side. **RIGHT** Wrong side.

PHOTO 2 Side seam in stockinette. An edge stitch is worked on every row. The first stitch is purled and the last stitch is a twisted knit (k1tbl). **LEFT** Right side. **RIGHT** Wrong side.

When sewing a seam on ribbing, plan the work so that the stitches match at the side and the ribbing flows uninterrupted. For a side seam with 2-2 ribbing, there will be differences in the look depending on how you chose to place the stitches at the side. You can either place a knit line of stitches inside the edge stitch on all sides, or two knit stitch lines at each side of the front and two purl stitch lines at each side of the back. The seam will be less visible if you chose the latter alternative.

When working in seed stitch (British moss stitch), make sure that a knit stitch meets a purl stitch at the side seam. Sew into the center of the edge stitch on top of the "ridge" on every row, which, in actuality, means on every other row. Make sure that the patterns match. Sew into every little upwards-pointing stitch on the right side.

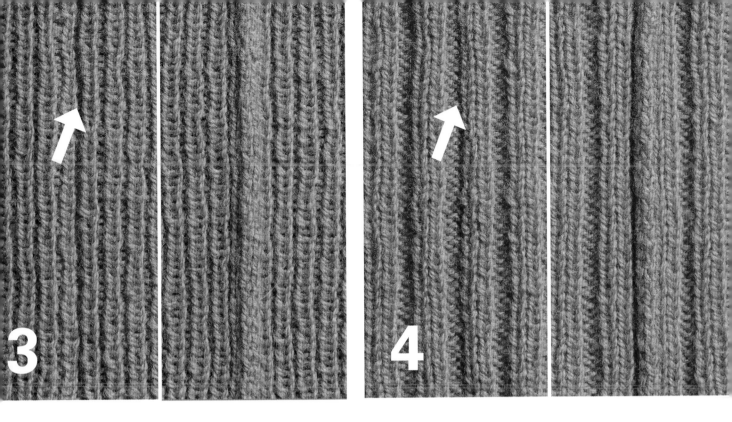

PHOTO 3 Side seam in 1-1 ribbing. An edge stitch is worked on every row. The first stitch is purled and the last stitch is a twisted knit (k1 tbl). **LEFT** Right side. **RIGHT** Wrong side.

PHOTO 4 Side seam in 2-2 ribbing. An edge stitch is worked on every row. The first stitch is purled and the last stitch is a twisted knit (k1 tbl). **LEFT** Right side. **RIGHT** Wrong side.

PHOTO 5 Side seam in seed stitch (British moss stitch). An edge stitch is worked on every row following the pattern sequence. **LEFT** Right side. **RIGHT** Avigsida.

PHOTO 6 Side seam in honeycomb. **LEFT** Right side. **RIGHT** Wrong side.

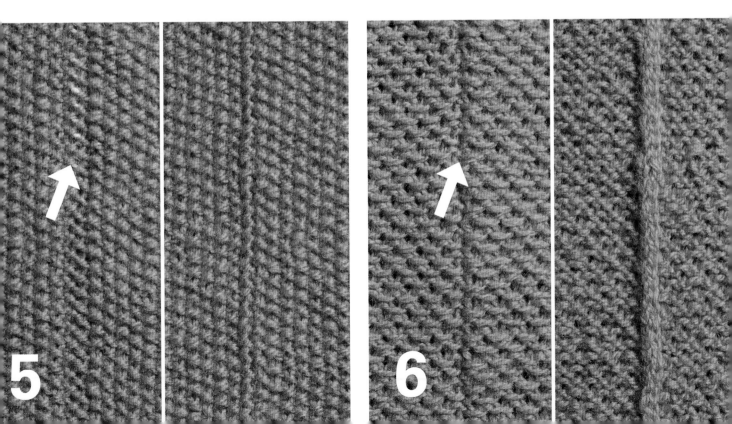

Kitchener Stitch

Learning to graft with Kitchener stitch is absolutely necessary if you want to master the art of finishing. Kitchener stitch is used to join two pieces of knitting, such as a shoulder seam or attaching a drop shoulder sleeve.

Kitchener stitch is also used for lengthening a garment where it won't do to knit in the opposite direction because of the pattern. The extra length can be worked separately and then sewn on.

Sometimes an edge on a neckline is knitted and then sewn to a row of picked-up stitches to achieve the absolutely most pleasing and harmonious completeness of the garment.

Estimate four times the length of yarn as for the width you'll seam and use a blunt, bent tip tapestry needle.

Think about ...

* When two pieces of knitting, each worked in the opposite direction, are sewn together, there will be a half-stitch jog, so it's always a good idea to include an extra stitch on, for example, the back shoulders.

* When casting on stitches and knitting a separate neckband on double-pointed needles, the number of stitches picked up around the neck and on the piece to be attached should be the same. See more on page 110.

KITCHENER STITCH FOR STOCKINETTE

When grafting two pieces of stockinette with Kitchener stitch, you should begin by binding off all the stitches with mercerized cotton yarn or work a few rows with cotton waste yarn to finish off. The bind-off or the extra rows will help you keep the stitches in place and hold them open and easily seen to be sewn into. When the join has been finished, you can then remove the bind-off or extra rows and see what a fine and neat seam has been formed. After you've become comfortable with the technique, you can leave the live stitches on the needles or slide them over to a length of yarn. Just make sure that the stitches aren't twisted when they are sewn.

For a shoulder, the stitches of the back can be bound off with the yarn that you have been knitting with. In that case, the bind-off will

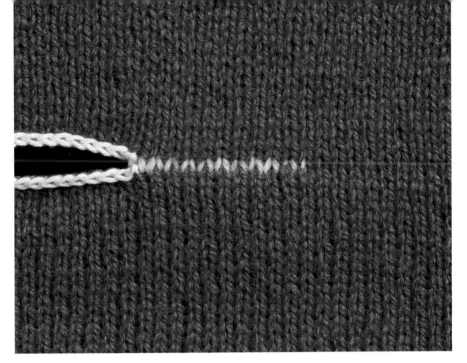

Stockinette. Open stitches on both pieces. One stitch less on one piece.

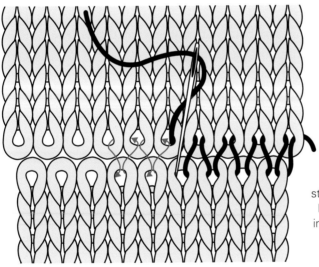

Stockinette. Kitchener stitch is worked into the live stitches. The grafting forms a knitted row.

remain when the finishing is done to reinforce the shoulder seam (see page 99).

After binding off, lay the two knitted pieces (most easily referred to here as the front and back pieces) flat with the right side up and with the stitches aligned with each other. The back, with an extra stitch, is further away from you. Place a sketch with the sequence of the grafting in front of you on the table. Insert the needle from below and upwards

Stockinette and reverse stockinette welts—three rows of each technique. The live stitches of both pieces. Kitchener stitch is sewn into a "row change" so that the knitting will match. In this case, rows of the reverse stockinette is the part sewn.

into the edge stitch on the back. Bring the yarn through and do the same with the edge stitch on the front piece.

Now make a stitch from the top and down into the edge stitch of the back while at the same time inserting the needle from below and up into the adjacent stitch on the back; pull yarn through. Do the same on the front. Tighten the yarn at the same time as you are sewing so that the stitches form a row that will look just like the knitted rows. Continue sewing, alternately into the stitches on the back and on the front.

It's important to make sure that you insert the needle into the *center* of a stitch. That way, the grafting will form stitches that will match the natural slant of the knitted stitches. If, instead, you insert the needle between two stitches, the grafting yarns will lie more parallel and "the row" of Kitchener stitch will not look very good.

If you have the misfortune of sewing between two live stitches, you just have to re-start because when the yarn or bind-off is removed, the stitches will drop.

A good mantra to recite while you are working Kitchener stitch with stockinette is: "down into an old, up into a new, down into an old, up into a new. "Old" refers to the stitch you most recently inserted the needle up into.

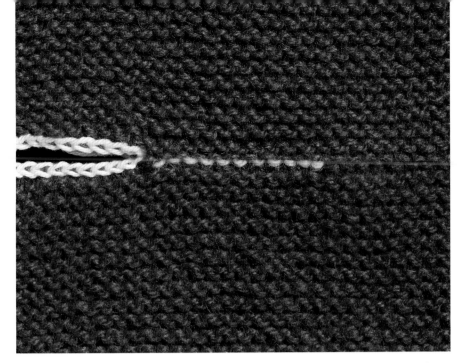

Garter stitch. Live stitches on both pieces. An odd number of rows on one piece and an even number of rows on the other. The grafting stitches are sewn so that the ridges in the knitting align.

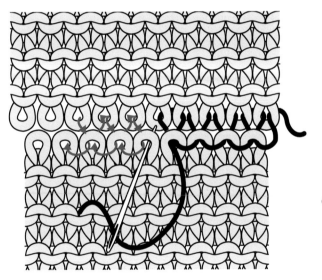

Garter stitch. Kitchener stitch worked into live stitches. The sewing forms a knitted row.

KITCHENER STITCH FOR GARTER STITCH

When garter stitch knit pieces are to be joined, work one piece with an *even* number of rows and the other with an *odd* number of rows so that the join will match on the ridges. The stitches on one piece are then sewn from below and up into the first stitch and from the top down into

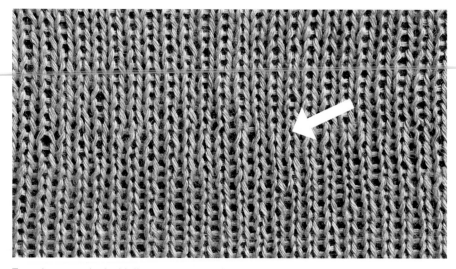

Two pieces worked with linen yarn and grafted with live stitches. The almost invisible shoulder seam is great for a summer linen with drop shoulders.

the second stitch. On the other piece, the sewing sequence is the same as for stockinette (see above). When the work is in front of you, it will be easy to see the grafting sequence so that the pieces will align.

Kitchener stitch is a fantastic technique that is unbelievably useful, but, because it isn't always easy to sew, there are many who hate the thought of it. If you feel that way, don't give up! Make another attempt. Knit two swatches with a light color, somewhat heavy yarn. Work for a couple of inches / a few centimeters, and, then, continue with a contrast color yarn, preferably mercerized cotton (which will be removed later on). Follow the instructions above for either stockinette or garter stitch swatches. Use a third, contrasting color, yarn to make it easier to see the Kitchener stitches. If you still think it's difficult, set the pieces aside and take a break—but don't give up!

Think about ...

✳ If you think it's hard to see which stitch you last inserted the needle into, hold a length of contrast color sewing thread with the grafting yarn. When the seam is finished, you can simply draw out the sewing thread.

✳ It's important that the grafting stitches be tensioned equally and neatly as you sew. It's hard to adjust the stitches afterwards because the yarn often "sets" itself.

Shoulders

A sweater can be made with either straight or sloping shoulders. Straight shoulders are always paired with drop shoulder, straight top sleeves that are attached with Kitchener stitch grafting. There are several variations, such as saddle shoulders or a sleeve, that are bound off diagonally instead of being bound off right at the armhole. The diagonal, shaped shoulder is always worked for a shaped sleeve.

The technique you'll need for attaching the sleeves depends on the type of garment, the pattern and the proposed wear. Heavier and larger garments generally have drop shoulder sleeves. Garments that are more form-fitting, a little thinner, and finer garments, usually have shaped sleeves. Vintage garments are most often knitted with shaped sleeves. Raglan sleeves are another option but their popularity is determined by the fashion world. Another type of sweater is the yoked sweater. Swedish Bohus sweaters are a fine example of that.

STRAIGHT SHOULDERS

When making a sweater with straight shoulders, it's a good idea to bind off the stitches on the back with the working yarn and to maintain the same tension as for the rest of the knitting after blocking. The bind-off should remain to reinforce the garment because, otherwise, the sleeves can pull the shoulder seams down.

The back piece should have one more stitch than the front because there will be a half-stitch jog sideways where the stitches with different directions are sewn together which is the case when front and back pieces meet.

The stitches on the front can advantageously be bound off with contrast color mercerized cotton yarn and then sewn, stitch by stitch, to the back. The cotton yarn is then removed. If you don't want to bind off the stitches of the front, you can place them on waste yarn or work a few rows with waste yarn which will be removed later or leave the live stitches on the needle, but the advantages of binding off—or working a few extra rows—are many. The stitches remain open and clear to be sewn into and you have no needles to slide out and fall onto the floor.

When you are working with thin yarn or using large size needles for tops or linens, you shouldn't bind off. In that case, it will be best if the

Straight shoulder. Stockinette. The back has one stitch more than the front and is bound off while the front has live stitches. The pieces are joined with Kitchener stitch that corresponds to a knitted row. **TOP** Right side. **BOTTOM** Wrong side.

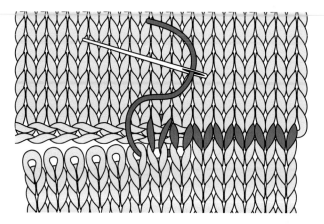

Straight shoulder. The back is bound off while the front has live stitches. The pieces are grafted with Kitchener stitch. The grafting forms a knitted row.

stitches are grafted when they are live on both the back and front pieces. That way no unattractive edges will be visible through the knitting. The shoulder seams will blend neatly into the rest of the knitting.

SHOULDER SEAM

Estimate four times the length of the seam for the grafting yarn. Use a blunt tip tapestry needle and sew the stitches to form a knit row. See more in the section about Kitchener stitch on page 94.

If you know that you'll have difficulty seeing the stitches, carry a contrast color sewing thread with the sewing yarn. That will make the grafting easier and, when it's done, you just have to draw out the sewing thread.

EXAMPLE 2 • You have 23 stitches and 29 rows per 4 in / 10 cm. If you sew one stitch to one row, there will be 6 rows left over. That means that you have to sew one stitch to two rows 6 times. Divide 29 by 6 and you have 4.8, rounded to 5. The number 5 means that, on every fifth row in the repeat, you need to sew one stitch to the fourth and fifth rows at the same time.

You can, instead, divide 23 by 6 for a result of 3.8, rounded to 4. The number 4 means that every fourth stitch in the repeat should be sewn to two rows.

Sew * 1 stitch to the first row, 1 stitch to the second row, 1 stitch to the third row, and 1 stitch to the fourth and fifth rows at the same time*. Repeat * to *. The ratio is 4 stitches to 5 rows per repeat.

Use the examples above when making your own calculations. Sometimes you might hit a problem and then have to think about how to solve it practically. Outline the number of stitches in 4 in / 10 cm as vertical lines on a piece of paper and then draw the number of rows in 4 in / 10 cm as horizontal lines to one side. Make sure you can find a pattern between the stitches and rows.

The primary consideration is that the division should be as even as possible and as alike as possible within each 4 inches / 10 centimeters.

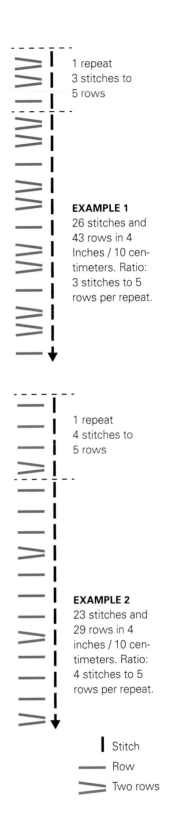

1 repeat
3 stitches to
5 rows

EXAMPLE 1
26 stitches and
43 rows in 4
Inches / 10 cen-
timeters. Ratio:
3 stitches to 5
rows per repeat.

1 repeat
4 stitches to
5 rows

EXAMPLE 2
23 stitches and
29 rows in 4
inches / 10 cen-
timeters. Ratio:
4 stitches to 5
rows per repeat.

| Stitch
— Row
Two rows

Picking Up and Knitting Stitches

Sometimes you need to pick up and knit stitches along a knitted edge. Perhaps you are working a sleeve out from the side of the garment or making a band around a neck or a button band on the front edge.

To pick up and knit stitches along an edge and have the edge even and fine, you need a foundation which is an edge stitch worked on every row (although there are exceptions). Just as important for a good end result and an even tension is that you know the ratio between stitches and rows in the knitting you are working on. That means how many stitches and rows are in 4 x 4 inches / 10 x 10 centimeters (see page 108).

If you decide to knit the sleeves from the top down on straight needles, you should consider adding an edge stitch at each side and finishing with a sturdy bind-off. You should also be aware that the knitting won't always look alike when the body and sleeves are worked in different directions. Various types of pattern knitting are good examples of this.

On the sample shown here, the ratio is two stitches to three rows. To help you see this, every third row has been marked with a cotton yarn—for each marked repeat, two stitches should be picked up.

PICKING UP STITCHES

Hold the yarn as usual in your left hand on the underside of the piece and use the right needle to pick up stitches along the edge, inside the edge stitches. If it's difficult to catch the yarn, use a crochet hook the same size as for the knitting needle and make sure that the stitches are not twisted when transferred to the needle.

In the example described here, with a ratio of two stitches for every three rows, pick up one stitch on the first row, one stitch on the second row and then skip the third row. The yarn on the underside floats once under one bar and twice under two bars (see drawing on page 112). Double check the stitch count to be sure it matches your calculations before you begin knitting.

PICKING UP AND KNITTING STITCHES AROUND NECK AND ARMHOLES

When picking up and knitting stitches around the neckline and armholes, use a smaller needle for picking up than the size for knitting the

TOP Stockinette with a ratio of two stitches to three rows. The rows are marked in pairs of three and three. The stitches are picked up and knitted in the opposite direction and marked afterwards as two and two which exactly matches the rows.

BELOW Shaping around the neckline at the same time as picking up and knitting stitches (marked only on the left side). The vertical stitches are picked up inside the edge stitches. The horizontal stitches on the diagonal are picked up in the stitch below the bound-off edge.

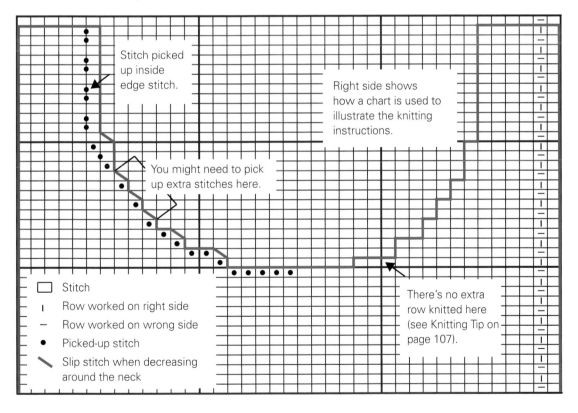

Stitch picked up inside edge stitch.

You might need to pick up extra stitches here.

Right side shows how a chart is used to illustrate the knitting instructions.

There's no extra row knitted here (see Knitting Tip on page 107).

☐ Stitch
Ⅰ Row worked on right side
‒ Row worked on wrong side
● Picked-up stitch
╲ Slip stitch when decreasing around the neck

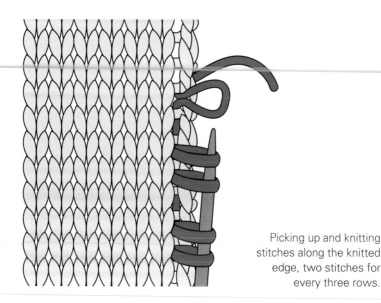

Picking up and knitting stitches along the knitted edge, two stitches for every three rows.

bands. The smaller needle makes the picked-up row tighter and so the garment will have a sharper and more even delineation between the edge and the body.

Hold the yarn as for regular knitting on the underside of the piece and use a knitting needle to help pick up the stitches.

In this example, two stitches are picked up vertically for every three rows but this can vary and it depends on the gauge of the garment (see page 25). Horizontally and along the diagonal, the stitches are picked up stitch by stitch. It's important to pick up stitches in the stitch itself, *not* between two stitches. Don't be lured into inserting the needle into a stitch below the bound-off row—it's easily done but it means the new stitch will lie between two stitches and break up the line between the stitches on the body and those for the neckband. In addition, the stitches will lie parallel, which makes for a less pleasing appearance.

Sometimes, you might have to pick up a few more stitches along a diagonal to avoid holes in the knitting. If necessary, you can decrease away those stitches on the first row of knitting.

Make sure the stitch count is correct for your neckline or armhole. It shouldn't be too wavy or too tight.

Neckbands

Neckbands should harmonize with the neckline below on the body and the bands around the armholes so that the garment will have an aesthetic whole. Begin by seaming the shoulders and then pick up and knit stitches around the neckline. Before you start knitting, make sure that you have the same number of stitches on both sides of the center stitch on the front and back. Also make sure that the stitch counts are a correct multiple for the repeat on, for example, ribbing. If you have too many stitches, you can decrease as needed on the first row.

If you are working a ribbed neckband, it will look best if the ribbing stitches are centered on the front and back and align with the rib stitches on the lower edge of the body, with knit over knit and purl over purl. This is of the utmost importance if you are working with a heavy yarn because the ribbing is so prominent.

If you've chosen to knit a stockinette band around the neck of a sweater or around the armholes on a vest, it will look best if you purl the first row on the right side before the stockinette begins. This row adds an extra bit of finesse. The purl row also diverts the eye from any unevenness in the knitting. The same advantage of the purl row applies even when you are working a ribbed neckband.

Another way to make an especially fine transition from the neckline to the band is to bind off the stitches on the first row and, with the same working yarn, pick up and knit the same number of stitches around the neckline. Pick up and knit the stitches in the back of the stitch loops of the bind-off edge. This will make a fine edge that looks like stem stitching (see pages 45 and 100).

It's easiest to work neckbands in the round with a circular or double-pointed needles. The neckbands described below were all worked in the round unless otherwise specified. Sometimes that means that you have to purl a row or work a knit row to get the right effect. Garter stitch in the round is worked by alternating knit and purl rounds.

If you decide to work the neckline back and forth, make sure that there's an edge stitch at each side to use as a seamline later on. The seam should be aligned with a shoulder seam.

When completing a standard bind-off around a neckband, knit the first stitch (the one that was knitted first and slipped over the second stitch of the round) and then pass the previous stitch over the new one (see drawing on page 132). This makes a very nice finishing for the bind-off row and makes it easy to fasten off the yarn end.

In an extreme case, to align the lower edge and the neckband, you can work the neckband separately. Cast on and work the band the same way as for working it directly onto the body or armholes. Sew on the band with Kitchener stitch to a row of stitches picked up and knitted around the neckline. Make sure you have the same number of stitches in the separate band as on the neck.

If you don't want any special kind of neckband, as, for example, on a summer linen, you only need to finish off the edges around the neck and armholes smoothly. One option is to pick up and knit stitches around as usual and then bind off on the first row/round. Sometimes, it might be necessary to work one row/round in stockinette before you bind off. This discreet edging harmonizes the garment in a pleasing way and is especially appropriate for inelastic yarns such as linen.

DOUBLED NECKBANDS

When making a doubled neckband, make sure that the facing which will be sewn down on the wrong side is the same length as the outer band on the right side. One section of the band shouldn't be larger than the other. Check carefully and remove or add a row as necessary (compare with the lower edge of the garment, page 66). If, for example, there are ten rows including the cast-on row before the foldline (a stockinette

Neckbands (opposite page)

PHOTO 1 Garter stitch edge, the first round is purled and bound off with the one-over-two method. Garter stitch in the round, alternating knit and purl rounds. The last round before the bind-off is purled to make a distinctive finishing.
PHOTO 2 The first round is purled on the right side. K2, p2 ribbing. Twisted bind-off.
PHOTO 3 K1, p1 ribbing starting on the first round. Bind-off over two rows.
PHOTO 4 The live stitches are bound off on the first round. The same working yarn is then held to the wrong side and new stitches are picked up and knitted in the back loops of the bound-off stitches. K2, p2 ribbing. Standard bind-off.
PHOTO 5 Rolled edge. An even number of stitches around the neckline. Six rounds for the "roll" and then stockinette for ¾-1¼ in / 2-3 cm so the smooth side rolls out towards the right side for a natural rolled edge. Standard bind-off.
PHOTO 6 Stitches picked up and knitted around the neck and then bound off on the next round. Linen yarn.

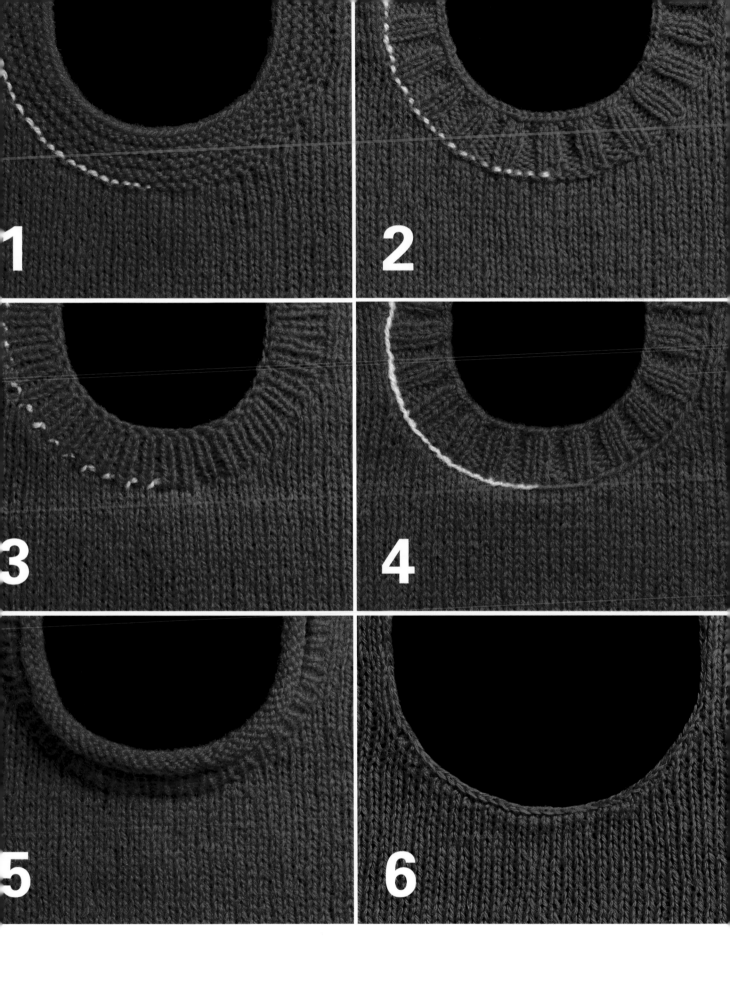

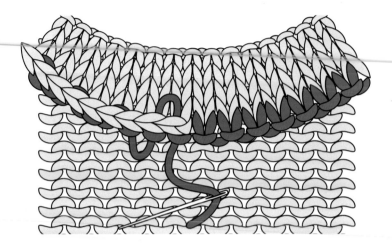

Doubled neckband. The left side was bound off and sewn down with blind stitch (compare with Photo 3 on opposite page). The right side was not bound off but sewn with Kitchener stitch into the live stitches (compare with Photo 1 on the opposite page).

row worked on large size needles), you should work the same number of rows after the foldline. If you decide to attach an edge with Kitchener stitch, the sewn row corresponds to the tenth row—which means you'll work only nine rows. If the foldline is a purl row, include that row with the edge folded to the wrong side.

If you choose, instead, to bind off and sew the edge to the pick-up row, work 10 rows after the foldline and then bind off. With a purled foldline, work 10 rows, including the foldline before binding off. Sew down with blind stitch. This stitch looks like a snake encircling itself.

To make it easier to see where you should sew the edge on the wrong side, hold a contrast color length of sewing thread with the yarn when you pick up and knit stitches around the neck. The sewing thread is removed after finishing.

When you've knitted a doubled band and are going to turn it down, you might want some reinforcement, depending on how the band looks. Deep, wide rounded and square edges sometimes have a tendency to be too flexible. To adjust for this, bind off the stitches instead of working a foldline with a larger needle and then pick up and knit new stitches into the stitches below the bound-off row. If you want a distinct foldline, pick up the new stitches in the back loops of the bound-off row. If you prefer a purled foldline, bind off the row following the purl row and

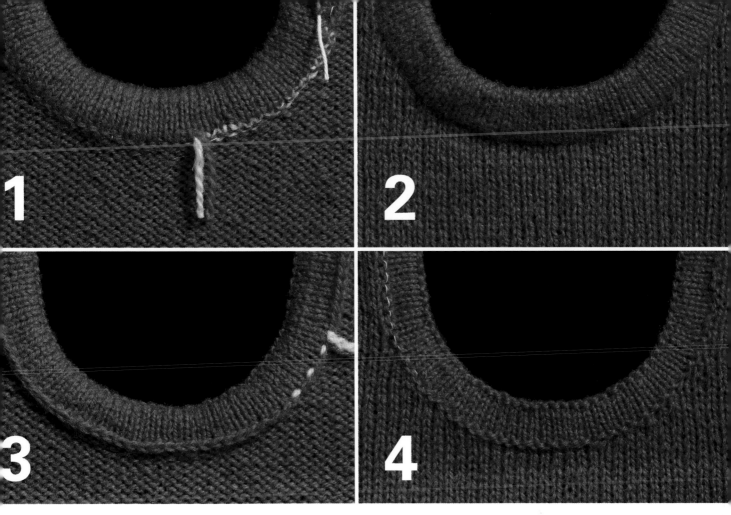

PHOTOS 1 AND 2 A contrast color strand of sewing thread is held with the working yarn when picking up and knitting stitches. A doubled band with a stockinette foldline knitted on a larger needle. The edge is sewn down with Kitchener stitch.

PHOTOS 3 AND 4 A contrast color strand of sewing thread is held with the working yarn when picking up and knitting stitches. The first row is purled. A doubled band with a purl foldline. The bound-off edge is sewn to the pick-up row with blind stitch.

then pick up and knit new stitches in the stitches below the bound-off row so that the purl row is retained.

Think about ...

✳ No matter what method you use to sew the edge down on the wrong side, you shouldn't be able to see the edge stitches or the bound-off edges on the inside of the neckband. The folded edge hides any unevenness.

✳ Make sure that the folded edge doesn't bias when you sew it down to the wrong side. There will be a half-stitch jog sideways.

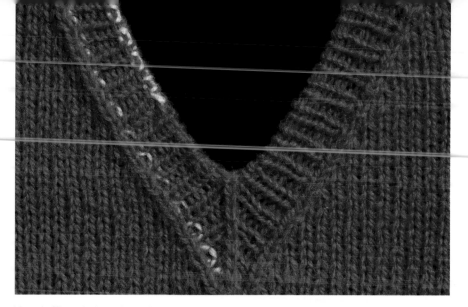

V-neck. The stitches along the edge are picked up and knitted inside the edge stitches of the body so that the "decrease" stitch line, the second stitch line from the edge, makes a distinct line. Finished with two rows of double knitting, one row on each side. Sewn bind-off.

RIBBED V-NECK BAND

Pick up and knit stitches along the neckline (in this example, two stitches are picked up for every three rows and the center stitch is on a holder, see page 104). When a row is skipped, the yarn for picking up floats behind the skipped stitch. **NOTE**: Now pick up and knit a stitch in both of the increased stitches (the edge stitches) on each side of the center stitch.

Make sure that there are the same number of stitches on each side of the center stitch. It's also important that the stitches on each side of the center stitch are worked alike—that is, to mirror image. If you are working in k1, p1 ribbing, you need to have an even number of stitches around the neck.

NOTE: Decrease one stitch on each side of the center stitch on every round by worked a double decrease so that the center stitch stays at the center. If you are working back and forth, make sure that the decrease on the wrong side mirrors that on the right side, with the center stitch still centered (see page 85).

Make the neckband as wide as you like (the last row can be worked as double knitting, one row on each side; see page 53) and then bound off with the sewn bind-off.

If you decide to work in double knitting, work the decrease so it lies on a knit stitch on each side of the center stitch and then decrease on

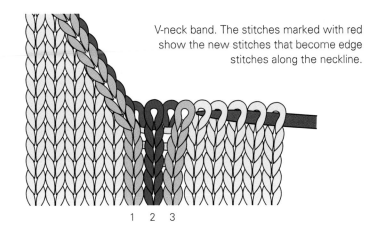

V-neck band. The stitches marked with red show the new stitches that become edge stitches along the neckline.

1 2 3

the first double-knitted row. On the next row, slip the center stitch. This way, you won't have to decrease when sewing the bind-off.

If, instead, you sew the bind-off edge directly after a ribbed row, make sure that there's a knit stitch on each side of the center stitch because you'll need to decrease even on the bind-off row. Arrange the stitches and bring the needle through all three stitches at the same time.

SQUARE NECKBAND — SINGLE LAYER

Pick up and knit stitches along the sides, inside the edge stitches. The number is derived from the ratio between the stitches and rows. At the center front and center back, pick up and knit a new stitch for each stitch (pick up in the center of the stitch, not directly below the bound-off row; see "Picking up and knitting stitches on the side," page 110).

A simple stockinette neckband finished with standard bind-off.

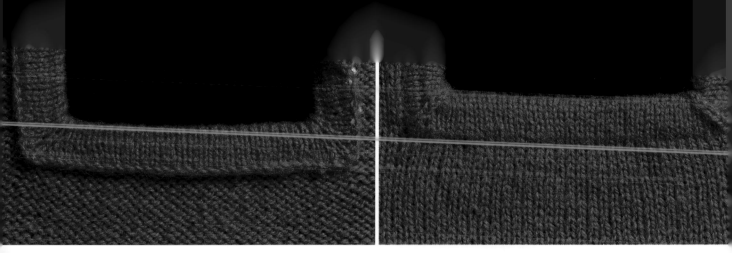

Doubled neckband in stockinette. The foldline is a bound-off row. The edge is bound-off and sewn down with blind stitch.

Make sure you add a new stitch at each corner—this stitch will be the center stitch at each corner when you decrease.

Work stockinette in the round. Decrease one stitch at each side of the center stitch by working a double decrease (see page 85). Decrease on *every other round*, including the bind-off row. Bind off.

SQUARE NECKBAND—DOUBLE LAYER

Cast on and work as for the single layer square neckband but hold a contrast color strand of sewing thread with the yarn when picking up and knitting the stitches. Work until band is desired with, bind off, but *do not cut* the yarn. Pick up and knit new stitches into the *stitches below* the bound-off row. Binding off adds stability to the garment; otherwise, the band could be too flexible. When the band is folded to the wrong side, the bound-off edge should fold precisely at the foldline, face towards the wrong side and be invisible.

Work the inside of the band. Increase on each side of the center stitch at each corner, on every other round. Increase with M1 in the strand between stitches.

When you have the correct number of rows and stitches on both sides of the foldline, bind off with cotton yarn and sew the edge down with Kitchener stitch (the row of Kitchener stitch corresponds to the last row; see page 94). Sew into the stitches of the pick-up row marked with the sewing thread. Make sure that the stitches are centered on each other and that the edge lies smooth and even. The cotton yarn and sewing thread can now be removed. Alternately, you can bind off and sew the edge down with blind stitch and then remove the sewing thread.

Setting in Drop Shoulder Sleeves

If your garment has drop shoulder sleeves, it will fit better if the sleeves are slightly set in on the garment. The armhole opening will be wider and there won't be so much excess material to take up room and feel bulky. Estimate about ¾ in / 2 cm for a child's garment and up to about 2 in / 5 cm for a large adult on both front and back.

To set the sleeve slightly in to the garment, bind off a number of stitches at the underarm of the body. The bind-off should match the rows at the sleeve's side seam. You can easily calculate how many stitches to concern yourself with if you know the gauge of the actual garment. The top row of the sleeve that will be sewn to the bind-off in the body should be knitted straight, without any increases.

For a better fit, set the sleeve a little in towards the garment

CALCULATING THE NUMBER OF STITCHES AND ROWS FOR AN ARMHOLE

In order to calculate and sew on a drop shoulder sleeve, you need to know the gauge in 4 inches / 10 centimeters for the piece as well as how many stitches and rows are in 4 x 4 in / 10 x 10 cm. You *always* have to know these numbers when you are knitting a garment. For that reason, before beginning a garment, you simply must knit a gauge swatch (see page 25). Once you know the gauge, you can calculate the ratio of the stitches and rows (see page 108).

SAMPLE • The ratio in the book's example is 2 stitches to 3 rows. 13 x 2 = 26 stitches. 13 x 3 = 39 rows. 1 repeat = 2 stitches and 3 rows. Start with the number of stitches at the top of the sleeve or the given measurement of the armhole depth in inches or centimeters and then make your own calculations. The number of stitches at the top of the sleeve = 98 stitches. Subtract the edge stitch at each side = 96 stitches.

How many rows are needed on each side of an armhole? 96 stitches divided by 2 (the count in the repeat pertaining to the number of stitches to make) = 48 repeats. 48 repeats x 3 (the count in the repeat pertaining to the number of rows to make) = 144 rows around the armhole. 144 divided by 2 = 71 rows on each side of the armhole.

If we work from the opposite direction and start with the number of rows in the armhole: 72 rows on each side of the armhole x 2 = 144 rows all around. 144 rows divided by 3 (the count in the repeat pertaining to the number of rows to make) = 48 repeats. 48 repeats x 2 (the count in the repeat pertaining to the number of stitches to make) = 96 stitches + 2 edge stitches = 98 stitches at the top of the sleeve.

This means that you would work 72 rows on the back and bind off with the standard method using the same yarn as for the knitting.

On the front, work 71 rows, bind off with cotton yarn which you'll later remove when you seam the shoulders with Kitchener stitch (see page 99). The joining row will the the 72nd row on the front which means that you now have 72 rows on each side of the armhole.

In case your calculations starting with the stitches and rows results in an uneven number of rows, work the front and back with the same number of rows. The shoulder seam with Kitchener stitch will provide the final, even-number row.

ATTACHING SLEEVES

First seam the shoulders. The back will have one stitch more than the front. Mark the exact center of the sleeve—there should be the same number of stitches on each side of the marker. The yarn for sewing up should be four times as long as the circumference of the sleeve. Make a slip knot to mark the center of the yarn and attach the sleeve with Kitchener stitch. Sew one side at a time, starting at the shoulder seam and the center of the sleeve. Use the half of the yarn strand for the front side of the sleeve and the other half for the back side of the sleeve. Sew inside the edge stitches.

In the example here (with two stitches for every three rows): first sew around one bar, and the second time, around two bars. Sew so that the stitching forms a knitted row. Tension the yarn as you work. In practice, this means that you are sewing around all the bars and will produce an even and fine stitch line.

When you get to the corner of the armhole, you must make one stitch into the edge stitch on the sleeve, turn and, in the same way, sew the sleeve's rows to the bound-off stitches of the body. The rows and stitches now lie in another direction. Continue sewing into the edge stitches on the sleeve. The little stitch in the edge stitch are not visible but will secure it.

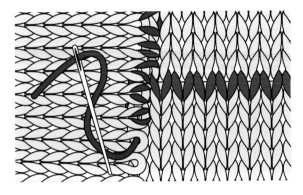

Attaching a drop shoulder sleeve. The seams are sewn with Kitchener stitch. There will be a half-stitch jog at the center of the shoulder seam.

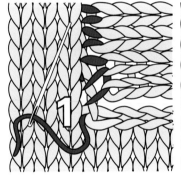

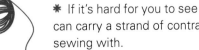

Sew with Kitchener stitch to the corner of the underarm. The stitch catches the edge stitch and the bar at the bind-off row (1). Sew around the bar made by the Kitchener stitch inside the edge stitch of the sleeve (2). Insert the needle into the same place on the body where it had previously come up and continue up into the stitch on the body (3). Sew the same way along the armhole (4), (5).

Think about ...

* Always sew inside an edge stitch on both front and back.
* If it's hard for you to see where you made the most recent stitch, you can carry a strand of contrast color sewing thread with the yarn you are sewing with.

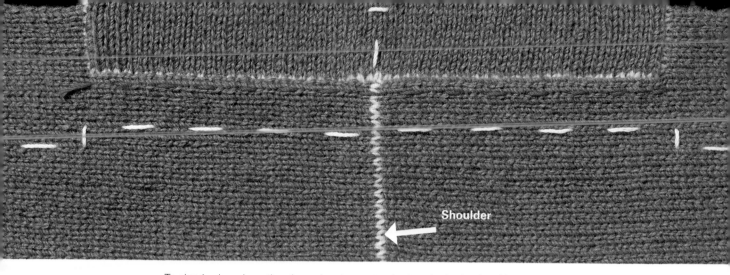

Shoulder

To clearly show how the sleeve has been attached to the body, the side seams have been ripped out and the sweater turned sideways at the shoulder seam. The red thread markers on the body show the number of three-row repeats, beginning at the shoulder. The white thread markers will help when you need to count the number of rows in the armhole.

Turn the work, release the slip knot on the yarn and sew the other side of the sleeve the same way. The sleeve seam will be neater when you sew one side at a time. If necessary, you can adjust the lower part of the armhole from both directions. Sew inside an edge stitch at each side; the adjustment of a half-stitch jog at the shoulder seam won't be visible (see Kitchener stitch, page 94).

Sew to the point where the seams meet each other at the center of the sleeve, thread the working yarn to the wrong side and fasten off.

MARKING THE NUMBER OF REPEATS IN AN ARMHOLE AS AN AID

If you have trouble keeping track of all the stitches and rows, you can mark the repeats. Start at the shoulder seam. Use a length of yarn to mark every third row (as in our example) on each side down to the bound-off row on the underarm; the bound-off row should be included in the count. Start at the center of the sleeve. In our example, for each repeat of three rows there are a corresponding number of repeats with two stitches (see the ratio between rows and stitches, page 108).

If the number of rows and stitches in 4 in / 10 cm varies in your knitting (the repeat in this case), you can mark the rows in the armhole. Begin at the shoulder seam and mark half the number of rows on the back and then the front, including a half repeat on each side of the shoulder seam. In the same way, mark the stitches of the sleeve top, beginning at the center.

Set-Up Rows

Set-up rows can be worked to make a clear delineation in a striped ribbing or for a smooth transition in a banded stockinette pattern with several colors. It can also be the first row after the cast-up edge or the last row before you bind off, if the cast-on or bind-off is worked in another color.

BANDED STOCKINETTE WITH COLOR CHANGES

If you want to knit a striped pattern in which you use both sides of the stockinette and bands of alternating knit and purl sections in combination with two colors, you'll get a dotted stripe with every color change, once on the front and next on the back. You can magically eliminate these dots on the front by working two rows the same way, one after the other, at the same time as you change the contrast color. This is called a "set-up" row. This technique can, for example, be used for knitting edges and turtlenecks on sweaters and cardigans, or on the brims of hats, on mitten cuffs, and sock legs.

The smallest number of rows for an effect stripe is two. Make sure the yarn at the side for the color change is always twisted in the same direction so that it will look neat. Two examples are described below:

EXAMPLE 1, STRIPING WITH FOUR ROWS • Work three rows in stockinette with the main color, beginning with a purl row on the wrong side.
*Change to the contrast color—on the right side—work 2 knit rows, 1 purl row, 1 knit row.
Change to main color—on the right side—knit 1 row, purl 1 row, knit 1 row, purl 1 row*.
Repeat * to *.
If working in the round, work 4 knit rounds with main color, 1 knit round, 3 purl rounds with contrast color*.

EXAMPLE 2, STRIPING WITH TWO ROWS • Purl 1 row with main color.
*Change to contrast color—on right side—knit 2 rows.
Change to main color—on right side—knit 1 row, purl 1 row*.
Repeat from * to *.
If working in the round, work 2 knit rounds with main color, 1 knit round, and 1 purl round with contrast color*.

Think about ...

* Maybe you'd prefer to use the wrong side with all the dots as the right side—in that case, you'll have a fine effect!

* When working in the round, you can avoid purling rounds if you work as follows:

With the main color, knit the desired number of knit rounds. Change to the contrast color and continue by knitting the first round (the set-up round). Turn the work inside out and knit in the opposite direction for as many rounds as you like. Turn the work out and knit in the opposite direction with the main color—you don't need a set-up round here. All the dots on the color changes land on the same side.

COLOR EFFECTS IN BANDED RIBBING

If you want striped ribbing with several colors, you can produce a fine, sharp transition between the stripes in which all the unattractive color dots are on the wrong side.

WORK AS FOLLOWS • Work the first row in stockinette with the new color. Work a knit or purl row over the entire row depending on whether you are on the right or wrong side. Knit the round if you are working in the round.

Work the following rows in ribbing. When it's time to change the color, repeat the first row in stockinette with the new color.

When working with a set-up row, the smallest number of rows for a stripe is two.

Make sure that the yarns twist in the same direction when changing colors so that it will look nice on the wrong side or at the side.

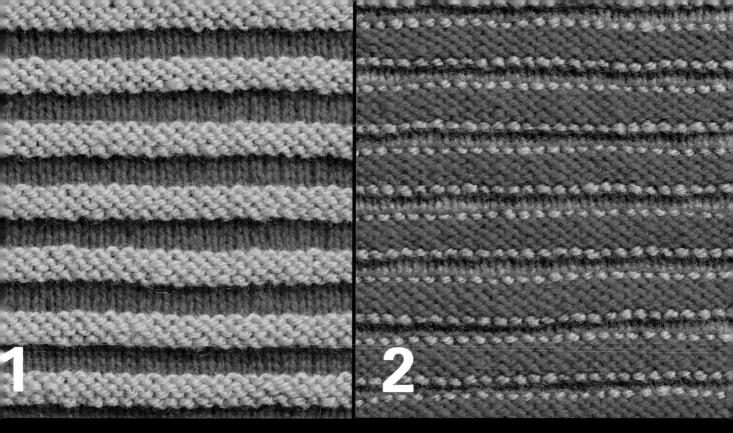

Set-up row

ABOVE Stockinette, four rows of each color. **PHOTO 1** No dots at all on the right side thanks to the set-up row. **PHOTO 2** All the dots from the color changes have landed on the wrong side.

BELOW K2, p2 ribbing, four rows of the main color, two rows in contrast color. **PHOTO 3** No dots at all on the right side thanks to the set-up row. **PHOTO 4** All the dots from the color changes have landed on the wrong side.

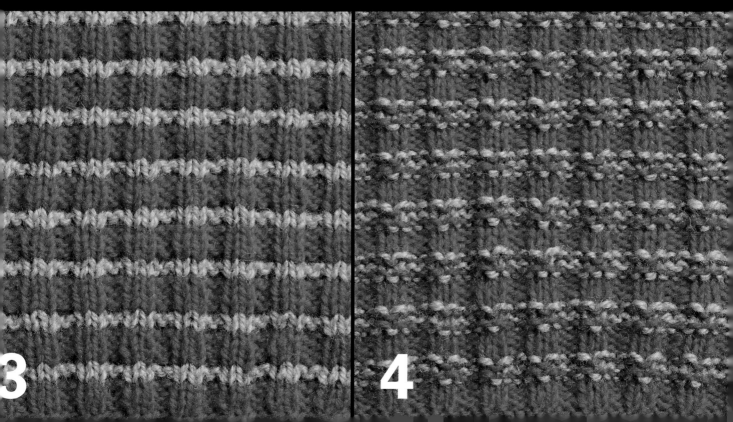

Short Rows

You'll undoubtedly recognize the classic little baby sweater that is worked from one front edge to the other with stitches cast on and bound off for the sleeves. It looks like a little fan and is worked in garter stitch with short rows. It's especially pretty when knitted with two colors. If you knit two rows of each color, you'll have a nice wrong side that you can also regard as the right side.

The term "short rows" refers to knitting only a part of a row and then turning. It can be worked without any unattractive holes in the knitting. In principle, the turns should not be visible on the right side.

A sloping shoulder can be advantageously shaped gradually with short rows instead of binding off stitches in stages with the ugly stair steps that follow. Even cowls, hats, tams, scarves, and large sweaters can be worked with the help of short rows.

The last stitch of a short row is called the "turning" stitch. If, for example, you plan on knitting a shoulder in three steps, the turning stitch is the last stitch in the number of stitches in each group given in the instructions.

WORK AS FOLLOWS • Work to the turning stitch, slip the stitch purlwise with yarn in front. Turn the work, slip the same stitch purlwise with yarn in front and work back across the row. At each turn, the yarn wraps around the slipped stitch. The stitch is slipped at both the beginning and end of the row to keep it open.

The turns are made the same way on both the right and wrong sides.

SHORT ROWS IN STOCKINETTE

Work a row over the stitches. When you get to the slipped stitch, catch the wrap *on the right side* and knit it together with the slipped stitch.

ON THE RIGHT SIDE • With right side facing, insert the right needle into the wrap from below and then directly into the stitch and knit the stitch and the wrap together. The wrap will automatically land behind the slipped stitch on the wrong side.

ON THE WRONG SIDE • With right side facing, insert the right needle into the wrap from below and then directly into the stitch and purl the wrap and stitch together. The wrap will automatically land on the wrong side.

Stockinette, a gusset formed with short rows in which the turns are made in the center of the gusset. The gussets are the same size on both sides.

It will be easier to work the stitch and wrap together if you first arrange the wrap together with the stitch on the left needle. Check to make sure that the joined wraps are not visible on the right side.

SHORT ROWS IN GARTER STITCH

When knitting garter stitch with one color, the turns can be made reversible by letting the yarn wrap around the slipped turning stitch, precisely as described above. When you work the next row, work the slipped stitch but *do not join* with the wrap. Pass them both to the right needle. Make sure that the tension on the yarn around the stitch doesn't pull in too hard.

If you are making a striped sweater, as, for example, a little child's sweater with vertical stripes, knit two rows of each color one after the other and then the color changes will occur at the lower edge of the sweater. The yarn you are knitting with lays over the waiting color. Tug the yarns so the color change will look neat.

It that case, it will look best if you wrap the turning stitch with the yarn as described above, lift up the wrap and knit it together with the stitch on the next row. The difference here is that you are always knitting on both right and wrong sides The same applies to a shoulder seam

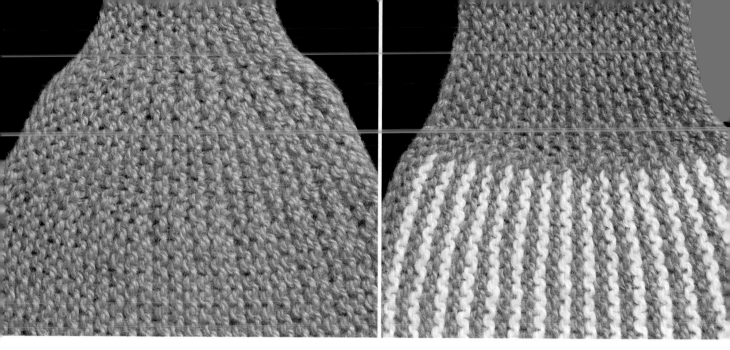

LEFT Garter stitch. Two turns. **RIGHT** Garter stitch with color effects. One turn.

worked with short rows and several colors. Just remember that the wrap should always land on the wrong side.

Garter stitch with two colors has an obvious right and wrong side but each will be fine and either can be considered the right side. In that case, it won't look good to have the wraps showing on the wrong side. If you want to have a definite right side, choose which side you want as the right side from the beginning.

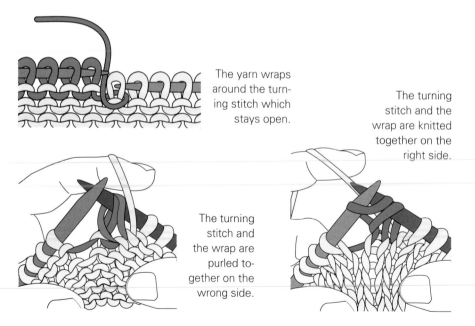

The yarn wraps around the turning stitch which stays open.

The turning stitch and the wrap are knitted together on the right side.

The turning stitch and the wrap are purled together on the wrong side.

Knitting in the Round

When knitting with double-pointed needles or a circular, it's easy to end up with a long strand between the first and last stitches when joining the stitches into a ring. Here's how to avoid that problem.

Casting on with double-pointed needles
Using the long-tail method, cast on, for example, 60 stitches with *one* needle. The right side of the cast-on edge faces you as you cast on the stitches.

Divide the stitches onto four needles as follows—16 stitches on the first needle, 15 stitches on the second needle, 15 stitches on the third needle, and 14 stitches on the fourth. The yarn that you'll knit with hangs from the 14th stitch on the fourth needle. Making sure that the row is not twisted, arrange the needles into a circle and slide one stitch from the first needle to the fourth. Now there are 15 stitches on each of the four needles. Begin knitting as usual with the fifth needle. See how easy it is!

If you start with a cable cast-on, then the yarn you'll knit with is on the other side. Cast on *one* extra stitch. Divide the stitches onto four double-pointed needles—15 stitches on the first needle, 15 stitches on the second, 15 stitches on the third, and 16 stitches on the fourth needle. Next, move the outermost stitch on the fourth needle onto the first needle (where the yarn you'll knit with is hanging) and knit both outermost stitches from each needle together. Now you can begin knitting as usual, with the fifth needle.

Casting on to a circular needle
Cast on an extra stitch. Making sure the stitches are not twisted, join the stitches into a ring. Knit the first and last stitches together.

KNITTING IN THE ROUND AND BACK AND FORTH IN ONE GARMENT
No matter what it says in the knitting instructions and no matter which knitting technique, you should never knit in the round up to the underarm and then work back and forth on straight needles. The result will

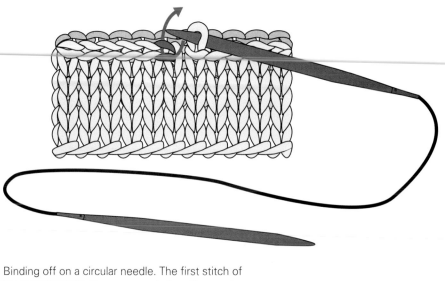

Binding off on a circular needle. The first stitch of the round is knitted once more before the previous stitch passes over it.

be an uneven piece because you are using two different techniques (only knit stitches when working in the round and then knit and purl stitches when working back and forth) and the yarns will behave differently. Even if you don't see the difference while you are knitting, the eye will notice the difference after blocking and when the garment is worn. So, work on a circular needle all the way to the shoulders and cut open the armholes and neck, or, work each piece separately. Let the camera be your extra eye.

KNITTING ON A CIRCULAR NEEDLE

If you are knitting on a circular needle, make sure that the needle is the right length to accommodate the entire piece out flat, not matter if you are working back and forth or in the round. That makes it easier to see the actual size of the garment and find errors more easily.

If you are knitting a hat or the fingers of a glove, it might be easier to use a very long circular and work with the Magic Loop method (see page 26). Make a sample first to determine the best knitting tools for your grip.

Performing a Magic Loop can be a good alternative to the short 16 inch / 40 centimeter circulars. Because the needles are short, they are hard to grip and your work will be uneven.

Two-Color Stranded Knitting

When constructing a pattern, you can draw it on graph paper, giving each color its own special symbol. Each horizontal row of squares corresponds to a row and each vertical row of squares corresponds to a row of stitches.

The chart is read from the bottom and up. For knitting in the round, begin on the bottom horizontal row of squares, starting at the right side. If you are going to work back and forth, read every other row of squares (the right side) from right to left and the alternate rows (the wrong side) from left to right, also from the bottom and up.

Two-color stranded knitting is best and most easily worked in the round on a circular, all the way up to the shoulder seams. You can knit the sleeves separately or do both at the same time.

No matter what it suggests in the pattern, do *not* work on a circular up to the underarm and then work back and forth on straight needles. This is in part because it's harder to knit more evenly and produce a fine pattern on the wrong side, and partly because everyone knits and purls differently, which produces varying results. Sample with some stockinette in one color and you'll see the differences.

If you are going to knit a garment in the round, also do the gauge swatch in the round using double-pointed needles or a long circular (see Magic Loop, page 26). If you are going to knit the garment on straight needles, then knit the swatch on straight needles. Simply said, knit the swatch(es) with the same style of needles that you'll use for the project.

When knitting with several colors at the same time, arrange the strands as usual with the help of the fingers on your left hand. The first strand, the dominant color, lays over the index finger and under the middle finger; the next color lays over both the index and middle fingers (nearest the nail). It's of the utmost importance that you *always* hold the yarns in the same arrangement throughout. Make a swatch with 1-1 stripes so you can see the difference if you hold the strands differently. If

Think about ...

... knitting both the body and sleeves from the bottom up. The pattern will look different if you knit from different directions. Compare the little lice in a lice sweater with the pieces knitted from opposing directions.

you are knitting two mittens to match and you change the arrangement of the colors, they will look different and, on a sweater, the knitting will also be uneven or totally reversed.

The yarn not being used for making stitches floats on the wrong side of the fabric. It's important that all the strands have the same tension as the rest of the knitting. You can catch the strand that floats with the knitted strand after approximately every third stitch. It's important that you look to see where the strands can be caught and also important that the twists do not land in the same place on every row because this can make ugly spots of colors showing through on the right side. Sample to see what gives you the best results.

If you are working back and forth, it's easiest to hold the yarns in the same arrangement even when working on the wrong side. On the wrong side rows, work with the right needle *behind* the strands and, when the strands need to be twisted, make sure that it doesn't show on the right side.

In a garment made with very heavy yarn, the strands can float loosely on the wrong side. When the garment is finished, working zigzag vertically by hand you can sew over the floats, catching each to the next stitch loop on the wrong side. Use a fine yarn in a matching color and quality.

Think about ...

... a small motif at the center of the piece can be easier to sew on afterwards with duplicate stitch. Another alternative when working small motifs on a single-color background is to work back and forth in a technique called "Intarsia knitting." Make a small butterfly with the pattern (contrast) color. At the color change, twist the strands of the main and contrast colors around each other. Work with the contrast color, twist the strands around each other again before the main color is taken up again with a new butterfly of yarn. In this case, the contrast color will not float on the wrong side of the work. Always twist the yarns on the wrong side.

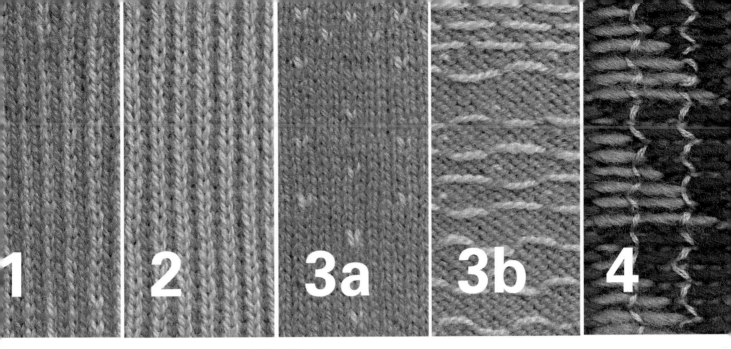

Two-color stranded knitting

PHOTO 1 Stockinette, one stitch main color, one stitch contrast color. The main color is dominant (see the arrangement of the strands on page 133). **PHOTO 2** Stockinette, one stitch main color, one stitch contrast color. The contrast color dominates (see the arrangement of the strands on page 133). **PHOTO 3A** Pattern knitting, right side. **PHOTO 3B** Pattern knitting, wrong side. The floats are caught on the wrong side in conjunction with the stitches. **PHOTO 4** Heavy knitted piece with the floats on the wrong side sewn down afterwards. The stitches are sewn loosely in zigzag so that they won't show on the right side.

NOTE: Half of the sweater; only the front has been worked.

PHOTO 5 An example of a sweater with the pieces knitted in different directions. Compare what happens with the pattern. The right sleeve is worked in the same direction as the body, from the bottom up. The left sleeve is worked from the top down.

The simple form of the pattern knitting has been combined with the edges worked in two colors and purl ribs. Cable cast-on. Neckband finished with one-over-two bind-off. The edges and the simple pattern combine well together and give the garment character. If a single-color ribbing were used for all the edges, the effect would be quite different and the garment would have less character.

A sweater knitted with a texture pattern for which the left sleeve is worked in the opposite direction, from the top down, in relation to the body and the right sleeve. Note the differences in the pattern and the edges.

Cable cast-on and one-over-two bind-off at the neck distinctively harmonize the garter stitch edges with the relief-stitch pattern. The first and last rows of the neckband are purled before binding off and the sleeves are sewn on with purl stitches.

NOTE: Half of the sweater; only the front has been worked.

Think about ...

... knitting all the pieces from the bottom up, all in the same direction, so that the pattern will be the same all over. If you knit the sleeves from the top down, the pattern on the sleeves will differ from that of the rest of the sweater.

Relief Stitch Patterns

Relief stitch or texture patterns are created with purl stitches on a stockinette background. The pattern is developed by either working knit stitches on the wrong side or purl stitches on the right side. A mixture of purl and knit stitches on a stockinette background produces many fine pattern effects and can also be combined with multi-color patterns. When working texture patterns, or relief stitch patterns as they are also called, you can use the same patterns as for multi-color knitting or cross stitch embroidery.

For a pleasing result, you should knit a little more firmly than for regular knitting—use smaller needles. The yarn should also be a bit "rounded" and not too soft. The pattern should stand out distinctly and it's likely that, in some cases, the patterns will be more obvious if you work back and forth—and not around on a circular needle. Wool yarn is excellent for knitting texture patterns.

Draw the pattern on graph paper with the horizontal lines of squares corresponding to a row and each vertical line of squares to a line of stitches. When working back and forth, read every other horizontal row (the right side) from right to left and alternate horizontal rows (the wrong side) from left to right. Charts are read from the bottom up.

SLIP STITCH PATTERN SWEATER

This red sweater has been worked in an old pattern, which is called "bird's feet" in Hermanna Stengård's book *Gotländsk Sticksöm* (Gotland Knitting). I want to show how important it is to think about giving a garment character with distinctive finishing. This is a pattern that flows.

At the bottom edges of the body and sleeves, the sweater has a simple cast-on and then a k1, p1 ribbed edge on the same needle size as for the texture pattern. The edge, 1¼-2 in / 3-5 cm wide depending on the size of the sweater, is folded under and sewn down with blind stitch which is not visible on the right side. This folded edge should not pull in the knitting at the bottom edge but, instead, reinforce the edge so it won't roll. For that reason, I've used a simple cast-on, which is very elastic, and then worked with the same number of stitches and same needle size as for the rest of the piece. Between the ribbing and the pattern there's a purl row for coherence and character.

Compare both sides

RIGHT SIDE The sleeves are attached with Kitchener stitch to form a purl row. The first row at the neckline is purled to add character and coherence and it also functions as a foldline. After the foldline, there's a ⅜ in / 1 cm stockinette edge that is folded under. The sleeve tops have a row of purl stitches inside the underarm bind-off row on the body. The same edges are folded under and sewn down with small stitches similar to duplicate stitch.

LEFT SIDE Note that the purl row at the top of the sleeve has been eliminated which means that the pattern has become mushy and extended. The distinctive finish has been lost.

NOTE: Half of the sweater; only the front has been worked.

Sweaters for Beginners

The sweaters shown here are the simplest imaginable for a beginner knitter or for anyone who likes an easy, pretty solution. The little details make these garments especially pleasing. The neckbands are matched to the edges on the body and the sleeves and the little details of the picked-up stitches all add up to that little extra something. The entire sweater fits within the circle. The neckbands are worked on a circular in the round.

Dive into your stash for some yarn and an easy basic pattern, knit the gauge swatch, and start playing.

SWEATER 1

Cast-on Long-tail

Technique K2, p2 ribbing and stockinette.

Increases Make 1 (knit into back of strand between stitches).

Edge stitches For stockinette and ribbing: purl the first stitch and knit last stitch through back loop.

Bind-off, Neckband Standard bind-off in ribbing.

The neckband begins with a purl round and then k2, p2 ribbing.

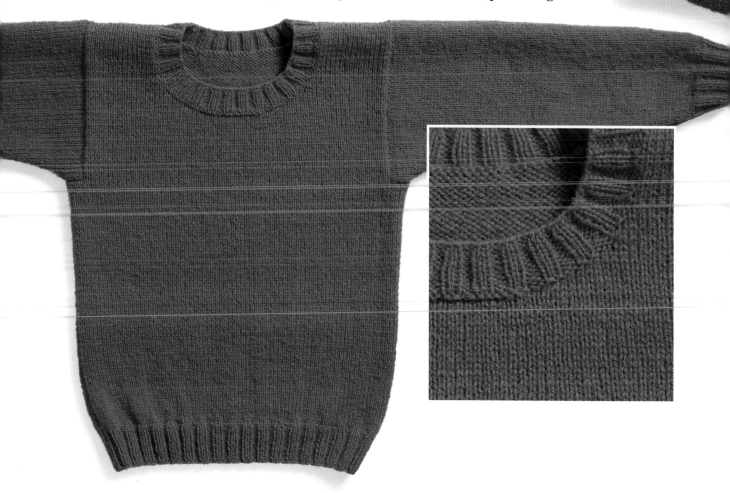

SWEATER 2

Cast-on Long-tail.

Techniques K2, p2 ribbing and stockinette.

Increases Make 1 (knit into back of strand between stitches).

Edge stitches For stockinette and ribbing: purl the first stitch and knit last stitch through back loop.

Bind-off, Neckband Standard bind-off in ribbing.

The stitches for the neckband are picked up and knitted and then first first row bound off with the standard bind-off method. Stitches are then picked up and knitted through the back loops of the bound-off row and followed by k2, p2 ribbing.

SWEATER 3

Cast-on Double Long-tail.

Technique K1, p1 ribbing, striped k1, p1 ribbing, and stockinette.

Increases Make 1 (knit into back of strand between stitches).

Edge stitches For stockinette and ribbing: purl the first stitch and knit last stitch through back loop.

Bind-off, Neckband Twisted bind-off on right side, with contrast color.

So the short turtleneck will fall in the right direction when folded down towards the front, the knitting is turned inside out immediately after the pick-up-and-knit row and then the collar is worked in the round on double-pointed needles. The inside of the collar is worked in a single color. When the collar is long enough, work the last round in stockinette with the contrast color as a set-up round before binding off.

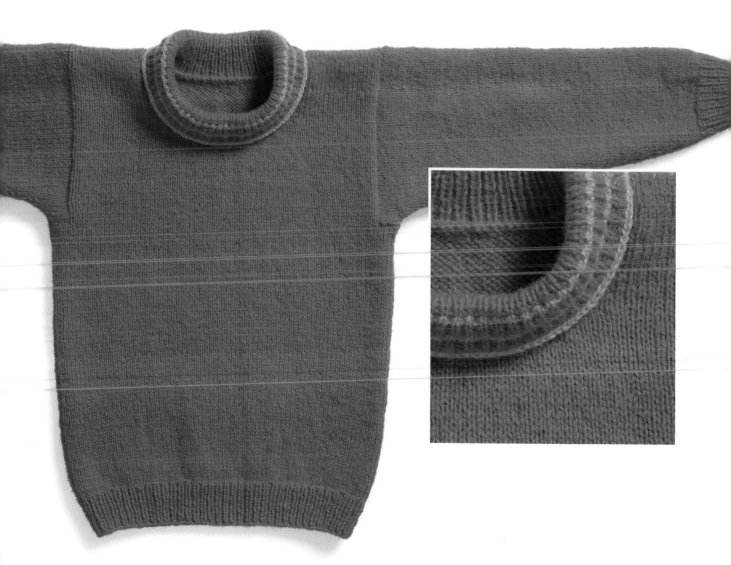

Garment Blocking and Care

Now you've knitted a garment with good quality natural materials. It has taken many hours but hopefully it has also given you peace and harmony. Knitting can, in many ways, be considered a form of meditation. You can sit for a while and let your thoughts fly away as you make stitch after stitch.

Many times instructions tell you to block the knitted pieces and then assemble them afterwards. You might also read that you should carefully steam press the pieces. I think this is totally unnecessary work. In fact, pressing can sometimes harm the surface and feel of the knitting. Many years of experience have shown me that the best results come from first assembling the entire garment and then washing it by hand. When you are knitting, you decide what the yarn will do; when the garment is washed, the yarn decides how it will behave.

WORK AS FOLLOWS • Set up some lukewarm water and add a little wool-safe soap. If the garment has been worked in bright colors, you might need to add a little white vinegar to the water—enough so the water tastes a little sour. The vinegar prevents the colors from bleeding and has the capacity to "lift" the colors and keep the garment from drying out.

Let the garment lie in and absorb the water for a little while but check to make sure the colors are not bleeding even with the vinegar. If the water turns colors, you need to wash the garment again without soaking it first. You can test the color fastness by soaking a corner of a white hand towel and pressing it to an inconspicuous spot on the inside of the garment. If the towel takes on color, then you should add the vinegar. Rinse the garment in the same temperature water as for the washing. Rinse until the water is completely clear. Do not use a rinse such as conditioner and avoid mechanical handling.

Let most of the water run out, carefully press out the remaining water, and then lay the garment out smoothly and evenly on a white clean and dry terrycloth towel. Roll up the towel as for a jelly roll, place it on the floor and then, very carefully, step by step, walk over the entire roll. Take out the garment, shake it and carefully stretch it as necessary and then lay it flat onto a new, dry towel. As it dries, lift the garment up, shake it, and turn it inside out while changing to another dry towel. Leave it until completely dry.

UNBLOCKED

BLOCKED

Hats, cuffs, mittens, and socks can all be blotted in and dried on paper towels. Change the towels regularly so the items will dry quickly.

If you follow these blocking suggestions, you'll end up with a pretty garment that will make a lovely overall impression. All the little details will harmonize well with each other. Don't forget, it isn't any trouble to hand wash.

Store knitted garments flat (but not in plastic bags) and air them out regularly.